WHAT I BELIEVE

Catholic College Students
Discuss Their Faith

WHAT I BELIEVE

Catholic College Students
Discuss Their Faith

edited by
David Murphy

THE THOMAS MORE PRESS
Chicago, Illinois

ISBN 0-88347-181-7

CONTENTS

Introduction

KARL RAHNER once wrote that every human being lives on the shore of the sea of infinite mystery, busy with the grains of sand that one finds there. In this statement he presents a blend of the mystery and reality that confront everyone in living out life in these latter days of the twentieth century.

The students whose papers are presented here have made an effort to identify this blend in their lives. Only a handful had been exposed to the new starting points of theology: personal experience and the human subject. Fewer were acquainted with the hermeneutic of Rahner's theology.

Since the majority of the students were juniors and seniors from the St. Mary/Notre Dame community, this represented for most of them the last opportunity to be introduced formally to some of the basic ideas that have become the foundations of our new understanding of theology.

Over the last eight years some fourteen hundred students have participated in helping outline a course that enables them to analyze and state their own experience on an individual basis. Each group of students generated its own chemistry, challenging one another and the professor, critical of some of the church's policies while probing and searching for meaning in their lives.

The basic framework of the one-semester course provided a dimension or perspective which would enable them to identify, understand and accept the implications of the new theology in their lives now—and, more importantly, some ten or fifteen years from now.

At the beginning of the course students were told that up to this point in their lives, they had been living mostly on the tip of an iceberg: that is, dealing mainly with the tangible, formal elements of their religion without sufficient understanding of why they believe the truths presented to them. The traditional propositional form of faith was alluded to in class as "the box," namely, the truths that were handed down and were to be believed on the authority of the church. Students then were invited to put on their scuba gear and, as a class, to dive down into the inky blackness at the bottom of the iceberg and there begin to feel, sense, experience the mystery found there. The questions arose: there is something here but what is it? What can we say about it? It is real, it is here, but what is it? Everything they had left on top of the iceberg was based on this.

By analogy, this experience of mystery was applied to the most basic questions of life: Who am I? What can I know? Why is there anything at all? Where do we come from and where do we go? Within this journey they began to recognize the search for meaning in their lives and the fact that somehow, someway, it was all connected with the mystery called God.

Once they accepted the idea of God as being the source of all reality—mother, father, friend—or, more simply, God as the meaning of 'who I am', they came to appreciate the qualities of transcendence and immanence in their lives and discover an openness within themselves which they experienced but could not fully explain. Thus their faith journey was enabling them to grasp more fully the mystery surrounding them.

From this point, following Rahner's thought, the students proceeded to internalize the concepts of faith, grace and revelation which led them to the study of Christology from below. The message of Jesus, the Kingdom of God, the meaning of his death and resurrection, and the faith experience of the first disciples after the resurrection leading to the community called church fleshed out the structure of the course.

Each week students were required to hand in a two-page reflection paper on some part of the lecture or class discussion or on outside reading they had done. These reflection papers became the basis for the final paper of the course: a ten-page statement of their own theology at this point in their lives. The two-page papers were corrected and handed back at the next class after the professor was able to analyze their understanding or misconception as expressed and then further dialogue toward understanding would occur.

These papers were marked on the basis of how well a student was able to express clearly his/her own thoughts. What they experienced and how they "theologized," even admitting to confusion and doubt, became the norm against which they were judged. Thus the method of simply repeating what the professor said or the textbook stated or what research revealed was of no help to them.

When it became clear to them that it was their own thought, their own reflection that mattered, they were faced with something of a problem. How does one tell a story about one's self? What are the right words to describe one's religious experience? Will parents and friends understand the doubts they have mentioned, the positions they have taken? It was at this point that learning became for them not a matter of facts or memory but a personal experience.

The Rahnerian terminology and understanding were presented to them as individual tiles with which they were to create their own mosaic: a picture of their relationship to God, Jesus Christ and the church at this point in their lives.

The fifteen papers printed here (two anonymously) were selected from among forty papers. Each one comes from a young woman or man who struggled to express the meaning of God in his or her life. Each picture is different. But behind each one you can sense the searching of one who is on a pilgrimage. Some of them are not in complete accord with traditional church teaching, but they are the sincere reflection of where these young adults stand now. They have confronted themselves at their deepest levels and have not hesitated to express gnawing doubts or unacceptable explanations.

The enduring quality of these papers is their truthfulness. They represent the first chapter of a spiritual autobiography which within a year or two has taken these students into the world of accounting, nursing, engineering, finance, medicine, etc., and into an atmosphere where they must account largely to themselves for the direction of their lives. Their problem will be to remain "hearers of the word" amidst a babel of tongues which will be confusing and at times inimical.

In his book *Concern for the Church,* Rahner forsees that the spirituality of the future is one that will be more lonely for and less supportive of the individual. He writes: In such a situation the lonely responsibility of the individual in his decision of faith is necessary and required in a way much more radical than it was in former times . . . . That is why the modern spirituality of the Christian involves courage for solitary decision contrary to public opinion.[1]

Compared to the experience of support and community which St. Mary's and Notre Dame offered to these students, his statement rings true. That is why at the end of the course each student was required to keep a xeroxed copy of the theological statement. They were told their mosiac was not quite complete, that some tiles would have to be replaced, their position rethought, a greater depth of color needed.

When this becomes an on-going experience, they will recognize that they are members ". . . of the poor Church of sinners, the tent of the pilgrim people of God, pitched in the desert and shaken by all the storms of history, the Church laboriously seeking its way into the future, groping and suffering many internal afflictions, striving over and over again to make sure of its faith."[2]

These students offer a picture of struggle and hope for the Catholic laity approaching the twenty-first century. It was with faith and with courage that they made their statements.

David Murphy, O. Carm.

1. Karl Rahner, *Concern for the Church* (New York: Crossroad, 1981) p. 152.
2. *ibid.*, p. 152.

STEVEN BOIE

AS a noted theologian, I'm often called upon to give my views regarding specific theological problems and issues. Unfortunately, however, this often causes people to lose sight of my overall theology because all they see are bits and pieces of the whole. To use a cliche, these people can't see the forest for the trees. What follows is an attempt to alleviate this problem, and allow people to see how my opinions on the specifics are merely projections of my conception of the whole. In other words, what follows is an attempt to explain my own personal theology. To better express my own theology, I will use the theology of Karl Rahner to compare and contrast my own theology. For easier understanding, this paper will be broken up into three different sections: 1) my conception of and relation to God, 2) my own Christology and how it affects or has affected my conception of and relation to God, and 3) an evaluation of the Catholic Church as it pertains to my theology and me.

Theology is defined in the *American Heritage Dictionary of the American Language* as "an organized, often formalized body of opinions concerning God and man's relationship to God." My definition of theology would be, "The expression of our relationship to God." In deference to this definition and the dictionary's definition, it would seem that the place to start my own personal statement of theology would be with my perception of and relation to God. I will try to do this without taking anything else into account. By this, I mean I will exclude everything, Christology, Catholicism, etc., and try to explain my relation with God in its purest and most unfettered state. This is much like what Rahner does in developing his theology. He takes the person, strips everything away, and starts building from there. This is in essence what I will attempt to do.

While I differ with Rahner on some things, I find that our conception of and relation to God are very similar. Upon studying Rahner, I found a name for many of the processes I have been undergoing all my life. Throughout my first twenty years, I've been aware of a void or abyss that seems to exist in even the happiest of times. I find myself asking the common question, "Is this all there is?" All humans go through this questioning, as it is the most basic, intrinsic line of questioning in man. I am constantly searching for meaning. It is in this searching that I can see God.

How is this so? Because in searching I transcend myself and go beyond the concrete realities of life to a place where I can at least glimpse the mystery that is called God. All my life this interaction has been going on. The use of the word "interaction" might not seem appropriate at this point, as the action I've been describing seems to be singular. However, God is also another important player in this drama. He is constantly revealing himself and in our transcending we are able to see him. Revelation is a unique experience for everyone. In considering revelation, I asked myself the question, "Have I experienced revelation, and if so, how have I experienced it?" The answer to the first question in my case is a resounding "yes."

My revelatory experiences haven't occurred because of my affiliation with the Catholic Church. The so-called "box" that has been handed to me by my parents, various priests, etc., really doesn't mean that much to me. I believe in God, but that isn't why. My revelatory experiences have come from two areas: 1) experiences of nature, and 2) personal relationships. A third area was mentioned in class, the working of our conscience and consciousness, but I feel this is just our interpretation of the first two. Right now I'd like to focus on the first area, experiences of nature, as I feel this area of revelatory experiences is especially significant in my life.

My home is located in a medium-sized town in the mountains of Montana. My particular town is surrounded on three sides by towering peaks, which afford me the opportunity to engage in my favorite pastimes: skiing and backpacking. While participating in these activities, I often see scenery that literally takes my breath away. This may be an overused, corny phrase, but in these cases it really applies. There have been times that I have had to use a snorkel to breathe while skiing because the snow was so deep and powdery it was literally suffocating. It's like skiing on air. There is a book called *Mountain Man* by Vardis Fisher in which the main character, a mountain man of immense stature, stands on the tip of a craggy peak in a driving rainstorm and sings—or considering his size, bellows—about his admiration, awe and respect for the creator of this awe-inspiring scene. I've had similar experiences. In these experiences, I seem to transcend myself and this world. In doing so I glimpse what I feel is an ultimate being or God. In gazing at these incredible vistas, I see beyond the physical to the metaphysical which I feel is God. No direct proof is necessary.

It is because of this revelation that faith is possible. As

Richard McBrien says, "This revelation is available in principle to everyone. All are called to salvation, but salvation is impossible without faith, and faith in turn is impossible without revelation." To me, faith is simply a belief and acceptance of God in one's life. It is the acknowledgement that God is there in all we do and that in all we do we must reflect this awareness.

This definition is very similar to another word that one hears repeatedly. This word is "grace." This term seems to me to be a sort of all-encompassing term. All of the topics I've discussed so far—transcendence, faith, revelation, etc., and the dynamic process that ties them all together, could be replaced by grace. Grace is the presence of God in our lives, and the way in which this presence affects our lives. We all have the ability to reject or accept this presence. Rahner uses the term "supernatural existential" to convey his feeling, which mirrors my own, that we have an infinite capacity to accept God. It is up to us to make that decision. It is here that I feel there is a paradox, for this all-important concept is not realized through monumental or noticeable things, but rather is reflected in everything we do. As Leo J. O'Donovan says in his book *A World of Grace:* "The fundamental way in which the offer of grace is accepted is genuine love of neighbor." The way we conduct our lives is in essence our acceptance or rejection of grace.

One thing I am adamant about in my theology is the genuine application of all these abstract principles to everyday living. One can use the words "revelation," "faith," "transcendence," "grace,", etc., all the time, but they must be applied. It is here that I feel the *persona* of Jesus Christ can enter the picture. He was the quintessential example of how one's life should be led. Jesus didn't just talk about faith, grace, etc.; he lived them. All human beings live them to some degree; but Jesus, a man who perfected the human, is the measuring stick against which we can compare our actions.

In considering Jesus, I must admit that I'm still unsure about many of the questions that arise concerning him. I will try to relay what I have definite opinions about. In my faith, Catholicism, the personage of Jesus forms a central figure upon which our religion and its basic tenets are based. Why this man is so important to so many people is a question that has popped into my mind more than once. Prior to this class, Jesus was a lofty character, much more divine than human. I was aware of God's presence in my life, but Jesus was a vague, almost mythical character. Jesus was a concept, or at least that is the word I would have used then, which I hadn't come to grips with. And that concept, to be quite frank, didn't mean a whole lot to me. However, since this class, I've gained new insight into Jesus and he has really begun to mean something to me.

The turning point in my consideration of Jesus came when I finally realized that he was wholly, one hundred percent human. I'd always been aware of his divinity, but this humanness added a new and meaningful twist. In reading *Jesus* by Donald Senior, I was struck by the concreteness of Jesus' life. It was amazing to me to see that he existed in a real time and place. Before, I perceived Jesus and the era and area in which he resided almost as if they were mythical, like J.R.R. Tolkien's Middle Earth. His humanness made his divinity much more appealing.

What made him divine? Jesus wasn't divine because God made him divine. God made Jesus human and Jesus made the human divine. Jesus was aware of a special relationship with God, but he didn't know he was divine. Because he was totally human, he learned about God through the same process as other people of his day. His relationship with God wasn't something that was innate in him, but rather it was a relationship that was fostered and nurtured as he developed in the culture of his time. In the case of Jesus, it reached a level that no other human being, before or after, has attained or will ever attain. Jesus accepted the totality of God's self-gift of grace. Or, as Rahner would say, he made complete use of his supernatural existential. He became divine by perfecting or redefining the human. Like all humans, he became aware of his inner secret or mystery at his death. In Jesus' case, this mystery, his own divinity, was revealed to him and his followers by his death and subsequent resurrection.

Personally, however, Jesus' resurrection doesn't mean as much to me as maybe it should. Paul says in his Letter to the Corinthians: "And if Christ has not been raised, our preaching is void of content and your faith is empty too. Indeed we should then be exposed as false witnesses of God, for we have borne witness before him that he raised up Christ; but he certainly did not raise him up if the dead are not raised. Why? Because if the dead are not raised, then Christ was not raised; and if

Christ was not raised, your faith is worthless.'' I don't feel Paul's statement is correct at all. I feel that Jesus' life and death are examples enough. By living the perfect life he did, and by dying the redemptive death he did, Jesus, I feel, was a revelation of God. This resurrection which is so all-important to Christianity, seems more like icing on the cake to me. In my mind, the resurrection is simply the realization that Jesus was divine. I'm not really sure if it ever really physically happened, or if it is just a symbol of the divinity of Jesus. This is one aspect of my personal theology that is still very unsettled.

Jesus, however, has now become for me another revelatory experience, to go along with the experiences of nature and interpersonal relationships. His life and death are an indirect proof of the existence of God. How could a human being like Jesus exist, if God didn't exist? The reason Jesus is so special, is that he is the revelation of God to all men. Other revelatory experiences are unique and not common to all. In Jesus, God has made his presence or offer of grace known to all men. To me, my newfound knowledge of Jesus has added a whole new facet to my religious experience. Sometimes in church, I can even understand what they are trying to say. Speaking of church brings me to my last topic: the church.

The Catholic Church has been a part of my life for as long as I can remember. My mother is a fairly devout Catholic; and every Sunday she made us go to mass, which was followed by a stimulating hour of CCD. (We went to CCD as we attended public schools.) I guess you could say that "the box" of beliefs that represent the Catholic Church has been thrown at me all my life. Unfortunately, I never knew what they meant.

This I feel is the church's fault. The church is becoming antiquated, and in my opinion Pope John Paul II is not helping matters any. John Paul II, as has been repeatedly pointed out on TV and in the press, is one of the most charismatic men ever to hold the papacy. But, looking past his public figure, I certainly don't feel he is infallible. His main fault lies in his and therefore the church's conservative, unrealistic stance towards important modern-day issues such as birth control and women in the priesthood. Much of the problem lies with the ethnocentrism inherent in the Roman Catholic Church. The key word here is "Roman," i.e. European. The Church seems to feel what is good for Rome is good for Nigeria or Chile or the United States. The Church seems to feel that the box which we refer to in class is the answer to everything and should apply in an identical manner to everyone.

What can be done about the church's tunnel vision regarding itself? Much progress already has been made because of Vatican II, but more is necessary. I feel that the church should slowly start adopting Rahner's method of theology. Instead of forcing the box upon its members, the church should attempt what we are doing in class. Examine the box from the individual's perspective and apply it accordingly. This of course would have to be a gradual process, but I feel it's definitely a necessary process if the Church is to remain influential in the lives of millions.

My reason for going to mass on Sundays is out of respect for God and not because I have any special feelings regarding the Catholic Church. I go to the Catholic Church because it's where I feel comfortable, but I don't feel it has a monopoly on being "the church." I'm sure some Protestant churches would suit my purposes equally well—as long as they aren't fundamentalist. My main criticism of the Church lies in the fact that I was never really taught why I was in church. Learning what I have learned this semester has made church much more meaningful (although it's still boring), as I can understand what the various prayers, creeds, etc., are saying. I'm actually starting to gain a sense of my Catholic identity. It's too bad I didn't learn all this earlier.

AL HARDING

LITERALLY, theology is the study of God; however, this understanding of theology is too cold and impersonal to capture the subsequent ideas of this paper. After nearly a semester of critical and reflective thinking, it is time for me to put it all together, to assemble the result of years of experiences into a structured format. Consequently, this will be a work of myself, reflecting the billions of experiences in my life that have shaped and are shaping my inner self as well as my outlook on the world.

I am a living document working out an explicit personal synthesis through the process of existential mediation. My faith has its origin in my personal experiences and is thus a personal faith. The resulting personal synthesis will be the interpretation of my faith, my personal theology rooted in the context of my life. It is not a stagnant, but a living, growing thing. My theology is evolving as am I.

Seeing that my personal synthesis reflects my experiences, I would find it appropriate to recall some of the more influential experiences of my life. From my parents I learned to follow a set of moral guidelines similar to the example of Jesus, but also to intellectually challenge the religious teachings presented to me. I had a difficult time developing a strong faith when so many intellectual gaps were present and I did not have the substance of character to pursue the matter. In addition, my previous Catholic education was just an education; the Catholic aspect was dead. I could not take other people as sincere in their faith when so much pettiness

22

and prejudice were present in a supposedly Catholic environment. In many ways, I had established a barrier that limited my relationship with God.

On the other hand, a Catholic environment is what I found when I stepped into the Notre Dame community. It is fitting that what so many people have coined "the Notre Dame experience" just happens to be the biggest depth experience of my life. It is an ongoing experience at the same time as I am reflecting upon it. I look around and see people who open themselves up to make true friends with others, people who extend themselves in countless ways to help those in need, people who appreciate the faith they have and are willing to have an open dialogue about their faith in the hope of promoting a growth of their faith. Above all, I remember attending a special mass and being in such awe when it was over, as if something had been ignited inside me.

What can I say about these experiences that will provide a clue to the context of my theology? Before coming to Notre Dame, my faith was floundering; I had no firmly rooted convictions of belief, but a set of moral guidelines. As a result, I brought with me no "box" of Catholic dogma that I was supposed to believe. Now, I am free to grow in the direction I wish and I am in a better position intellectually and emotionally to decide which direction. As a result of my Notre Dame experience, I have chosen a direction in which I can develop a personal relationship with God, a faith that will provide meaning in my life.

My life is a process. My experiences, actions and thoughts are a process of search for meaning in my life. Why am I searching for meaning in my life? I have a desire to find the coherence of all that occurs. I want to know for what purpose I am alive, to find a significance about my life. As a human, I inevitably search for an answer, whether the search is conscious or subconscious. I believe my meaning goes farther than my environment; it is God that provides my meaning. With God as the ultimate meaning, there exists a coherence for all the seemingly chaotic events of life. God is the answer for me as a human searching for meaning.

In recognizing that God is the meaning of my life, I have broken out of the circle of day-to-day concerns into a greater, less muddled recognition of God. I, myself, have made this realization of God as the meaning of my life. Thus, God is a part of my human experience. I believe, and it is an implicit part of an understanding of God, that God is transcendent. He does not exist in only my experiences but in everyone's; He exists not only in the outer realms of my experience where I can realize Him, but also in the inner realm of daily distractions where I have been blinded to him. His being transcendent throughout my experience, provides the meaning and guidance of my life. His being transcendent means He is part of everyone's experiences, and thus the ultimate meaning of everyone's life, the answer to being human.

In this light, several theological concepts that I once viewed as archaic and coming from the "box" are intimately a part of my human experience. What is it to say that God transcends my entire existence, all my experiences? What is it to say I can break out of the chaos of day-to-day activity and find a knowledge of God, to recognize there is one ultimate meaning, not an earthly one but an infinite one? I believe that this is to say that my existence, human existence, is full of grace. Even if I don't recognize it, God is present in all my experiences, infinitely extending His grace to me. However, my relationship with God is shaky because of my shortsightedness. I am not in constant union with God even though God is always extending His presence to me. I get bogged down in my daily activity and often fail to see that God is there for me to follow. This is my struggle for unity, to be a whole human, to be in touch with the meaning of my life, that is to say, to find salvation.

I have been expressing the need to recognize the meaning in my life. This seems, though, too intellectual. In addition to recognizing God intellectually, I can come into contact with God through faith and through my actions. If God is present in all my experiences, as I believe He is, I can unthematically respond in my actions. As long as I act with a concern for others and their needs, I am living a graced life, something I strive for because it means I have let God enter my life. So whenever I am puzzled, I ask myself what Jesus would have done; and when I falter, I tell myself that I did not treat my neighbor as Jesus would have. I can strengthen or weaken my relationship with God through my interactions with other people. I believe I can best strengthen my relationship with God by following the example of Jesus, for through Jesus' graced existence, God revealed Himself to me and to all humankind.

It is Jesus' human experience that provides concreteness of meaning to my day-to-day life. Otherwise, I believe my faith would be reduced to fragments, to the times when I take time to reflect. With the human example of Jesus, my daily activities are meaningful, and a product of my search for meaning in my life. For in the aspect that Jesus was human, had human experiences as I have human experiences, and yet was so very close to the meaning of human life, I find great hope. It was the humanness of Jesus, his subjection to temptations, drives, and anxieties, that makes his loving example so compelling to follow. In following his example, I am being guided to the meaning of my life through the medium of my experiences. My faith is not fragmented, but permeates both my intellectual and physical being; my faith is directional and pointed toward God, not something turned on and off like a lightswitch.

But Jesus was different from me. Jesus is the great example of life, the provider of hope, and God's revelation to man. I believe that Jesus' relationship with God was so strong that not only could he recognize God as the meaning of his life, but he led his life filled with this strength. It was Jesus' total acceptance of God's presence in his life that made Jesus divine. Being in such close touch with God, Jesus desired to teach and live out that which God desired, the Kingdom of God.

What is it about the Kingdom of God that caused Jesus' life to be dominated by it? Looking at the relationship between Jesus and God, Jesus was totally open to God, having strength in his actions and wisdom in his words. To me, Jesus was such a great man because his words and his actions were as one. He was living out the will of God; he was a part of the Kingdom of God and was helping others in their search for the Kingdom of God. It seems to me that the dominance of the Kingdom of God in Jesus' life reflects the will of God, progress toward the ultimate love, peace, and truth for man.

In Jesus' life, I see several aspects of the Kingdom of God. Jesus tried to make others aware of the nature and immanence of that Kingdom. I believe that in the miracles Jesus performed there was a message: God has power over all things, evil included. This power in conjunction with God's love and desire for our well-being points to the immanence of His Kingdom. Moreover, I believe I have come to an understanding of the nature of the Kingdom of God by understanding the actions of Jesus. In Jesus, the love and the sense of truth that I associate with the Kingdom of God are exhibited. These actions are a sign of a man at peace, a man who is secure with himself. I feel that Jesus reached God's kingdom as a man. In believing this, I believe Jesus' love and compassion came from a secure knowledge of the meaning in his own life which was inspired by grace. Jesus had a firm grasp on the meaning of his life; he obtained salvation through God's grace.

Yet, I am still struggling in a process of humanization, struggling toward security of meaning, struggling toward the destiny of the Kingdom of God. Jesus had found the security of meaning and was able to reach the Kingdom of God; Jesus was humanized, had obtained his full potential. In so far as I understand this, I understand what it means to believe that because Jesus was totally human he became divine.

I believe that God is present in all my experiences, that He sent Jesus as His revelation to provide an example and hope for me and all humans, that God's power and His desire for man's well-being will result in His Kingdom. But this is not a stopping point. If I really believe these things, it will show in my actions. If God is present in all my experiences, I believe I should reach toward Him in my own way, in so far as I can. But how do I bridge the gap between the mystery of God and the reality of everyday life that I search for Him in? I believe my faith provides the foundation for the bridge, and the framework is built as I follow the example of Jesus. As I struggle to follow Jesus' example, I am struggling to obtain peace, truth, and love in my life. I am attempting to achieve that lifestyle which God would have me lead; I am searching for the Kingdom of God in this respect.

To me, it is evident here how much sense all this makes. I am seeking a personal relationship with God, and as a human, I seek God through attempting to attain those qualities present in His Kingdom, through humanization. I, being human, am in a process of humanization and the level of humanization I obtain depends on the level of being human I grow to. This acknowledges various degrees of quality. Because I believe that God would not create one man more human than another, and yet that people do reach different levels of love, compassion, and truth in their lives, I must believe that I have an influence on and a responsibility for bringing about the Kingdom of God. I am able to decide what level of being human I obtain, how close I reach to God in my life.

In as much as this is important to me, I will strive to love others, to lead my life with a sense of truth and with compassion for others; and the example of Jesus will be the force behind me. However, there are evil forces in the world such as racism, obsession with one's state of well-being, and violence. I firmly believe, though, that the conditions of God's Kingdom will rise above these evil forces, and thus I should govern my life according to this belief, for this is how I reach out to God in my daily life. Those who are racist, I must love because they are human; but out of a sense of truth, I must hate that ideal which they hold. I believe I should frown upon governmental policies which benefit the rich and at the same time cut aid for the poor, for education, and for protection of our world's environment, because it is not in this way that the Kingdom of God will come to be. All possible efforts should be used to prevent war and violence and instead to search for the real truth. It is by no accident that the greatest man ever to live was a man of truth, justice, nonviolence, concern for the lowly and most importantly, love. It is Jesus' great example that motivates me to be a Christian.

I started this paper by stating that I am a document shaped by my experiences. After rereading this, my explicit personal synthesis, it only becomes more evident that what I believe and do are a product of my experiences. This paper is my theology; it is what I believe. I only hope that I find it important enough that it will be reflected in my daily life. I must struggle to make it so.

KATIE WHELAHAN

DEVELOPING my own theology has not been a process of learning to deal with "the box." Rather, it has been the gradual realization and expression of my previously undefined faith. Having no formal Catholic education or training, I used to feel that I might be missing some critical information or ideas and I was afraid to articulate my own beliefs for fear of being wrong. I no longer feel this way, however. It is clear now that formal religion only has meaning when it is based on a deeper understanding of its subject matter: God and Jesus Christ. As these have become real and meaningful to me, I have put together this theology. It is in no way complete, but I do not believe it should be. John Updike has written that theology must always unravel and be reknit. This allows us to reinterpret our faith whenever we feel it is necessary. I believe that my evolving interpretation will help me not only to understand the most basic meaning of God but also to deal with the questions I must face here on earth.

My most fundamental belief rests in my concept of God. I have no doubt that God exists because I feel that man would not be compelled to seek a higher being if He did not. As a child, I perceived God as a father figure, eternally good and wise, subtly providing me with authority and direction. In many ways, my perception has not really changed; I have merely added depth to my image as I have grown older. God is a *constant* thrust in my life, present at all times and in all experiences. God is not a static being but rather a flowing presence, evident upon close examination in everything I know. Therefore, I think it makes sense to say that God is the source, foundation, and goal of our being.

It is clear to me that a basic restlessness troubles human existence; all of our earthly accomplishments cannot prevent us from asking "Is this all there is?" Although each human being is unique, I think that each one of us shares a need to find some meaning in life. Also, I believe that each one of us is fundamentally directed toward God our creator and that God gives every human being the radical capacity to transcend his tangible surroundings in order to reach some under-standing of himself and of God.

Although we often become caught up in day-to-day activities, I believe that most of us yearn for trans-cendental experience because it lifts us from our human limitations and allows us to come closer to the source of our being. I suppose there are people who are frightened by the idea of universal meaning and who prefer to con-centrate on earthly life, but even they cannot escape transcendental experiences altogether because all human beings are forced at one time or another to confront matters such as birth or death which demand their atten-tion and reflection. In short, we all must recognize our mortality and the limitations it places on us. I believe that an understanding of this reality causes us to use our limited lifetimes to pursue the meaning we naturally seek for ourselves.

As I have attempted to do this, God has communi-cated himself to me through both individual and collec-tive experiences. I have become increasingly aware of myself; but like most people, I have not reached a point where I can make a conclusive statement about the nature of God. Rather, I have experienced awe, wonder, and even confusion at his endlessness. Nevertheless, I have come to understand that the better we understand ourselves, the better we understand God because He is the meaning of who we are.

This does not fully explain God, but I am satisfied with this definition because I believe that God is by nature a mystery to human beings. Even if I break away from the immanent level of my life and devote myself entirely to transcendental experiences, I can only realize the endlessness of His and hence my own meaning. I will never reach a final end or conclusive, universal statement of meaning because my most basic source of meaning, God, is incomprehensible to me now.

I suppose that many people turn to the Catholic Church for a concrete answer, but I have never really done so. Basically, this is because I have not had much exposure to the church as an institution and I do not really understand many of its facets. I believe that God is the ultimate end and that the church is capable of mediating God to man but not of establishing a relationship between God and man.

Since I have been at Saint Mary's, I have decided that the church's strength lies in its ability to provide a basic structure for our faith and beliefs. The Church also has value in that it establishes a community of human beings who are conscious of the presence of God in their lives and aware of their search for meaning. This allows us Catholics not only to share our beliefs but also to act upon them here and now, and in this way I believe we make our lives more meaningful. After all, temporal and proximate things are not necessarily meaningless and superficial; as human beings we are required to find meaning in what surrounds us in order to find meaning in greater things.

Nonetheless, I am somewhat skeptical of the church as the sole mediator of our theology. It seems to me that the church tends to over-emphasize dogma to the point that many of its members become angry. Certainly church leaders are thoughtful, educated men, but their perspective varies greatly from the perspective of most Christians. It is unreasonable to assume that they are capable of establishing a social structure or moral code which will allow all Christians to express their faith or beliefs in a manner which has meaning for them in their particular cultural context. Forcing people to submit to rules or conventions does not necessarily strengthen their relationship with God; instead, it alienates them and discourages them from developing in the community. I think it is very important that individuals integrate the dogmas of the church into their own personal understanding of God. Dogma's value lies in its ability to make an individual stop and think about an issue. It must not be presented as an indisputable truth that needs no interpretation to be relevant.

By now I suppose it is clear that I think every person's individual relationship with God is extremely important. I have thoroughly internalized Karl Rahner's concept of the fundamental option which states that a person's destiny is determined not by his individual acts but rather by his fundamental decision to orient himself toward or away from God. Once someone has made this choice, he must decide how to implement it in his life. This is not to say that sin is determined by the outlook of the sinner;

knowingly or unknowingly, we all commit sins of varying degrees of seriousness. It merely expresses my belief
that the most basic decision we make is also the most important decision we make.

This rather individualistic outlook does not prevent
me from placing a great deal of value on the mass.
Despite its relatively structured nature, I believe the
mass provides an excellent opportunity for people to
deal with the church on a personal level. Although I do
not feel that attending mass regularly necessarily makes
one a "good Catholic," I think it is essential that time
be put aside to pray and to reflect and weekly mass provides just that. It reminds us of the presence of God and
helps us to understand the person of Jesus Christ. Mass
is no substitute for faith and beliefs, but it is an excellent
outlet for them.

I realize that my professed Catholic religion is based
on Jesus Christ, but I must admit that the person Jesus
Christ has not been the cornerstone of my own faith.
Again, the basic reason is ignorance and misunderstand-
ing. It has always been difficult for me to accept the idea
that the historical Jesus is "The Way" and that those
who do not know Jesus as such cannot know God or attain salvation. Also, I have found the miracle accounts
to be difficult to believe, somewhat hollow, and basically an unsatisfactory source of "proof" of Jesus'
divinity. Although I have believed that Jesus was divine,
I have felt plenty of confusion over the how and why.

The introduction of the idea of Christology from below or ascending Christology has allowed me to develop
a much more meaningful understanding of Jesus Christ.
It is critical to accept the life of Jesus as a human life,

complete with doubts and struggles, because this makes him more relevant to all of us. We are better able to value his activities if we realize that Jesus did not have supernatural powers or an omnipotent capability to "fix" things through his lifetime. Nevertheless, as a human being he was extremely conscious of God and he became divine by perfecting this consciousness. It is clear to me that Jesus Christ symbolizes the self-communication of God and represents the potential capabilities of human beings.

Therefore, while I perceive God in almost metaphysical terms as my most fundamental or universal source of meaning, I understand Jesus Christ as holding real implications for my life here and now. I believe that as a human being, Jesus exemplifies how God would like us to live our lives, and the obvious presence of God in Jesus' life represents an ideal toward which we all may strive.

Jesus was undoubtedly human, but I think he was unique because he somehow realized a greater meaning than the rest of us. I do not believe that each one of us could perfect himself or herself to the extent that Jesus did; but I am confident that any human being is capable of finding the ultimate meaning of who he is and therefore reaching the point of salvation, where the purpose of both temporal life and basic existence are understood. Although I cannot be sure, I think that this occurs as an individual nears his death. I do not think that human beings should fear death, because I believe that only at the end of a lifetime can the individual truths experienced at various times and from many different perspectives become one comprehensive body of knowl-

edge. Also, my understanding of the resurrection gives
me confidence in life after death. Having already
established that Jesus was a human being whose life
symbolized the potential of man, I think it makes sense
to say that Jesus' resurrection represents an end which a
person can attain if he tries. Of course this is not to say
that each of us will arise as a divinity after death. What I
feel is that the resurrection represents God's forgiving
nature and willingness to accept us back into Himself
after we complete our lives here on earth, provided we
have made the basic decision to orient ourselves toward
Him.

This leads me to the idea of the evolution of the
world. I am convinced that the historical process moves
from the simple to the complex, and I can see a progressive development in individuals from unconsciousness to
consciousness to self-consciousness which suggests that
each human being is in the process of becoming, transcending himself so as to make himself more open to
God.

If one accepts a definition of God as the source, foundation, and goal of our being, it becomes clear that
God's self-communication has been present throughout
time. His presence has, I believe, guided the movement
from simple to complex. Human beings are always
evolving and developing, and associating God with this
process assures that there is no finite end to their evolution.

This process seems less clear on the level of the entire
world, however, as the issue of freedom becomes relevant here. I think that we often define freedom as the
ability to do whatever we want. However, a good deal of

human life is determined by forces other than the individual's demands, and therefore no one is completely free in his choice of actions. But no one is restricted at all from determining what he will be. To reiterate an earlier theme, God has created human beings such that each one of us can search for the meaning of himself and in the process reach some understanding of God.

This does not guarantee that all human beings will make the decision to do so at the same time, however; and the decision of each human being will be reflected in his actions. Although God's presence on earth is apparent to me, I have always believed that God created man and established standards for him but essentially left him alone to decide what he wanted to accomplish and how. Therefore, even though I understand that history progresses in God's presence, I find it difficult to imagine history following the same pattern of development that human beings follow. History consists of the actions of many individuals and each individual not only is at a particular personal level of consciousness but also is directed by his own free will.

However, I do not believe that God simply created the world and turned his back on it. I feel his presence here on earth and I believe many other people do, too. Our awareness gives us a sense of direction, and I have faith that we can co-create a world with God. I have come to understand God as the fundamental source of meaning in my life as well as the lives of others. The sooner everyone accepts this fact, the better it will be here on earth.

This theology has developed from a basic, unthematic knowledge of God which I have tried to refine and embody in a realistic, relevant statement. I think that it is a very basic interpretation, and I feel that I have much room for development, especially in terms of Jesus Christ and Catholicism. However, my basic faith in God gives me confidence in my capabilities, and I believe that I can continue to gain both a greater awareness of myself and a clearer understanding of the meaning of things around me, both immanent and transcendent.

SALLY WILLIAMS

*Writing this paper impressed upon
me my own inadequacy in dealing with God.
My words are stilted and never express
the depth or the feeling that I desire.
Just as I begin to tap into my own
theology, I realize that it is much more
than can be conveyed. I offer this:
a first attempt.*

THREE months ago I began this class believing in God
—not with any set proofs or theorems or just from
habit. I believed in God then, as I do now, because I
cannot believe in man. To rule out God is to confine
spirituality, any capacity for spirituality, to the finite.
The infinite, the mysterious, is necessary in my world
view to give meaning and purpose. Yet, I cannot help
but be overwhelmed by modern man's obsession to
define life in human terms. Twentieth century literature
is hauntingly desperate and barren. Suicide is an obvious
solution to man's futility. Trapped in a finite vision of
the world, man offers self-destruction rather than salvation.

I, on the other hand, am willing to believe in the
mysterious presence of God. I do not understand how or
why I am a receiver of his love and grace. But it is God
who gives me possibilities, who gives me hope when I'm
surrounded by insurmountable odds. Even the day-to-
day life of a student is wrapped in a web of despair as I
am faced with unresolvable issues: threat of nuclear war
and destruction, suicide, wide-scale starvation, eco-

nomic injustices. The love of God can break down the walls I'm building in the name of protection—walls that will "suffocate" life if they are completed.

So, I believe in God because I can't believe in a world with no God. My faith is a soul-wrenching belief that God exists and is active in my life—a theistic faith. And though it may sound like it, my faith is not founded on a hope or refusal to deal with death and mortality. My faith has evolved from experiences I've had—that is why I state so firmly that God is alive and active in the world, regardless of the evidence to the contrary.

My faith has been sustained through personal experiences, scripture and prayer, and the church. To offer a little background, I did not grow up in a traditional Catholic home. In fact, I've had more exposure to Jesus Christ from the reading of the Bible than from dogmatic teachings.

Basic to my theology is personal experience of the divine, the mysterious in my life. At certain points in my life, especially when I am unguarded and unprotected, I've felt a particular closeness with Jesus Christ. It seems that when I've suffered without understanding—as with the death of a family member—it's then that I've been most aware of God's presence. I can't explain this phenomenon: an experience of the knowledge that there is deeper meaning, an ultimate reality beyond the one I am able to comprehend. Even in the chaos and confusion, there is the peace and compassion of God's presence.

I have also had this sense in close relationships with other people, as if I'm scratching the mere surface of something great and unfathomable. The relationship taps and fosters expression of something greater than the two people involved.

At times I have the feeling that life, in itself, is a witness to the presence of God. When I stand on a mountainside in Colorado, the wind caressing the trees and whispering through the grass, creation seems to be in me and I in creation. We become the very expression of God.

This is not to say that I do not question and struggle with the issue of God in my world. But personal experiences, for me, tend to be *experienced,* taken for what they are, not really probed. They act upon me and are impressions that lead to further inquiry into the nature of God.

But it is personal experience that brought about the second phase of my faith—an active experience. As I came to an awareness of God, I began to want to know more about him, about my relationship to him. The natural place to turn was the Bible. At this same time, prayer, the need to practice prayer on a daily basis, came to the forefront. This was and is the most essential part of the building of my faith. It is here that I discovered and clung to the human Jesus for identification and reference. A prayer life and knowledge of scripture are the backbone and foundation for my theology. From them, I began to "theologize," to sort out my world from the perspective of Jesus Christ.

Two years ago, I discovered my faith on a third level: the church. This started my collective identity. Until this point I was focusing on myself—my responses, my par-

ticipation. Now I studied the teachings of the church for
the first time; and I realized the true nature of the sacraments, of the "Body of Christ." The church is a witness
to my faith; for in many of the teachings, signs, and
sacraments, she has embodied what I believe. I now express my faith through and in the Church, as well as
through personal experience and scripture and prayer.

It is important to note at this time that my theology is
a journey, an evolution. I know not what lies ahead, but
I know that it is a journey in exploration of Jesus. My
beliefs have been prompted and initiated by various conversion experiences, two of which I choose to discuss.
These aren't the definitive conversions in my life. There
have been many I am aware of and many I have not
been aware of. But these represent, in my mind, two
turning points.

My thematic experience of God, when I chose him,
came in my freshman year of high school. I was on a
retreat, meditating on the face of Jesus in a picture.
Sitting in the silence, I was touched in a very deep way
beyond the usual level of experience. I read the passage
in the Bible about being hot or cold, but not lukewarm.
I reviewed my life and realized that I was lukewarm. I
was straddling a "fence of faith." I was not happy and
knew that some decision had to be made then and there.
The eyes of Jesus spoke to my heart as if saying, "Sally,
I love you. I will be with you, but you must decide and
you must live with that decision." I made a commitment
that night to live *for* Jesus Christ. In my limited way
(limited by age and experience), I knew that life was
senseless and had no meaning except in Jesus. Eight

years later, I still hold to that decision. I have failed many times; I have been afraid of that failure. Yet, I'm consistently drawn back by what I understand life without God would be like: I see futility, despair, isolation, and death. I don't see any reason to live in a world like that.

This was a very individual experience, acted out in a personal way (development of a prayer life, etc.). But I was not satisfied and didn't know what was missing. My sophomore year in college, while I was studying in Rome, helped put the puzzle together even more. During a beatification mass at the Vatican, I turned around to a sea full of people. Seriously, all of Saint Peter's Square was packed, stretching down the street entrance. The fountains were obscured by the magnitude of the gathering. There were hundreds of countries represented and many people came in traditional dress. Throughout the mass, I was most impressed with what the church stands for and represents. I am Sally Williams, an American. I can travel to Rome, Italy or any part of the free world and still share in the same Jesus Christ that I share in at my home parish in Dallas, Texas. A collective identity in the church was awakened in me that day.

Personal identity with God is good and necessary, but strength and support come from identification with the whole Body of Christ. My life has more potential when I see it acted out in the power of the church. However, life cannot exist on this level alone. I need a relationship with God to balance it. Perhaps I've moved in a different direction than most—from a personal relationship with Jesus to an understanding of the church and what it represents. I am still a child in the church. I have an innocent delight in the prayers and sacraments because the experience is so new.

These two thematic revelations have been true depth experiences. My life has been altered and unified: growth in faith, knowledge, and integration of my relationship to God, man, and myself.

However, I stress that these haven't been the only conversion experiences. God has been and is active on a daily basis. I am the one who has the freedom to accept or deny his presence or assistance. Spirituality is painful, for it is never satisfied. Every time I seem to reach a goal, I have only come to a point where I see how far I am from God and from understanding.

I have come to accept many things about my life. I struggle with the issue of God and man, but sometimes the only response possible is acceptance. As my life is full of polarities, so is my faith. The tension of living with two opposites is a creative force. For example, I believe in God, in his presence, and his participation in this world. However, I am also aware of the hunger and exploitation that go on. Where do the two meet? How can I reconcile this so that I can live with it?

This may sound rather trivial and basic. But essential to my theology is paradox. Paradox, though painful, challenges growth. It admits limitations and challenges the foundations of my faith. Faith is believing without seeing, without touching. Whether Jesus rose corporeally or performed all the miracles is not fundamental. The presence of God is.

The two extremes of my spiritual life form a paradox. At times I experience a joy, a happiness, a satisfaction, a contentment with my life with God. I have a seeming union with all around me and the Creator. Believe me, this is where I'd like to stay. There is such peace and tenderness.

However, lately it seems I experience the opposite (which is difficult to see as spiritual growth). I experience a darkness, a dryness, fear, thirst and hunger. I am blind. My life is arid and I move, oh, so slowly. I am faced with my own inadequacies and the inadequacies of the world around me. Sin, being a state of humanity, and death are overwhelming. Much is irreconcilable, and faith is determination and perseverance. The only response I can muster is to turn to God with open hands.

I can't explain why I have grown to accept these things. Maybe it won't always be so. I believe, I have faith, and in faith I accept paradox.

This attitude acknowledges my responsibility. I recognize my participation in humanity as a reference point for my responses. But the here and now existence is the individual and immediate world. My life here demands some sort of action. My theology is founded in the collective and acted out on the individual. One cannot exist without the other. Faith and faith experiences, to be real, must reflect the experiences of the body and the message of Jesus Christ for his followers.

I know that the grace and mercy of God have been active in the world through salvation history. I've come to know it, ironically, through my own salvation, the way in which He has been active in the whole of my life and the lives of people around me.

My reconciliation of the two, the point where they meet, is in the Kingdom of God. I will be honest and say that this topic is difficult for me. The Kingdom of God is the recognition of my responsibility in the world. Faith and hope that the Kingdom of God *will* be a reality prod my lagging feet. At this point, I cannot see it. It seems as if man is hurling himself towards destruction. If I do not consent to believe in the Kingdom of God, I will have to accept defeat, failure, and senseless suffering as intrinsic to the world.

Perhaps the only time I've experienced the power of the Kingdom of God as a universal reality was at the beatification mass. Yes, I see the Kingdom of God acted out in the people around me, but that was a manifestation of God's power that overcame the barrier of culture, social class, etc. I needed to have an experience like that to strengthen my own search.

Contrary to this experience, my theology is acted out on a very small level. I work in the circle around me; most likely I won't affect multitudes. But I am contributing to the Kingdom of God as a whole, linking me with wide-scale human effort, faults and all. In the face of this, my search continues.

I've ended with many contradictions and my own personal confusion, but that is all I have to offer. And yet this is faith, this is theology. My God is large enough to encompass it all. In identifying with a very human Jesus, I've learned not to reject these feelings. I need to face them and deal with them the best I can. Doubt is not always destructive. In the divine Jesus, there is hope and inspiration that God does work in my life and the life of man. There is an end towards which we are moving. The presence of God in my world stops the headlong rush

towards self-destruction and offers salvation. I only
need to stop and listen for his voice in the midst of the
confusion.

> I said, "Ah, Lord Yahweh; look, I do not
> know how to speak: I am a child!"
> But Yahweh replied, "Do not say, 'I am only
> a child.' Go now to those to whom I send
> you and say whatever I command you. Do
> not be afraid of them, for I am with you
> to protect you—it is Yahweh who speaks!"
>
> Then Yahweh put out his hand and touched
> my mouth and said to me: "There! I am
> putting my words into your mouth. Look,
> today I am setting you over nations and
> over kingdoms to tear up and to knock
> down, to destroy and to overthrow, to build
> and to plant."
>
> Jeremiah 1:1-10

MAUREEN HARTNETT

IT is strange to think that there are probably as many different theologies in existence as there are people walking around in the world. Mine is unique to me just as every other one is unique to its holder. My own personal theology is something that is constantly progressing, more rapidly in recent times than before, and surprising me to some extent. One of the most definite things I can say about my theology is that it is based on my faith in God, not necessarily on my religion. In other words I do not identify with or totally accept any religion including the religion to which I belong. Rather, I choose to believe in and relate to God through my lifetime of experiences and without claiming any one institution or idea as "correct."

Before I began this religion class I had a fair number of notions in my head regarding my religious beliefs. Some of these notions were conceived from the "box" which I was brought up in—the Roman Catholic faith—and others were additions to or negations of my "box" which I had derived from getting older and experiencing more of life. Lastly, some were very recent conclusions I felt forced to reconcile myself to because of my father's death. As I said, these were *notions*, not concrete irretractable beliefs which I would have felt capable of or comfortable in defending. Sometimes when I thought about these notions I felt ashamed that my religious beliefs were not definite and matter-of-fact, but now I am beginning to realize that these notions are what the theologian Karl Rahner refers to as "the unthematic" and are not anything to be ashamed of.

48

I attended a Catholic grade school where I came to believe that my religion, with its belief in the Trinity and its own special celebration of the mass, was the chosen religion of God. Supposedly, Catholicism was the religion God wanted us to follow, even though Jesus was a Jew; and I accepted this. When I entered high school my religion became nothing more than a process of going through the motions, and by my senior year I had stopped going to church on Sundays. Even though I really enjoyed my senior religion class and tried to live my life following the teachings of Jesus on love and humanity, I was too caught up in my own little world to reflect deeply on what the real power and meaning behind this thing we call "life" is.

After another year of this sort of faith as a freshman in college, I began to realize in the back of my mind what had been going on in my life and what was coming at me in the future. It was no longer the world I had seen as a high school junior or senior with my rose-colored glasses. My future was at hand, the world was full of problems, and I would have to start taking charge and making meaning of my own life instead of always being directed. So in order to settle all this unrest within me I began to go back to church and, little by little, ask some questions to which, little by little, I found some possible answers.

I think actually that I began to collect these ideas in my head during my freshman year in college, and even moreso the first semester of sophomore year. I have come to believe that my Catholic faith is not necessarily the "right" religion, but rather something I was given at birth, just as I was given my name. Neither do I accept all the teachings of the Catholic Church. I think that if I were born a Protestant I would have kept that religion and not quibbled about it. I don't know if that is a terrible thing to say, but I think what is more important is how you live your life—not what you call yourself. I don't believe that anyone will ever know what the "correct" religion is or even whether there is one. The most concrete conclusion I have drawn is that I will never understand life or God, except perhaps when I die. It is this belief which I have, in a sense, resolved to accept in order to keep my peace of mind.

All of these notions, among others, have been present in the subconscious of my mind for a while, but I have never discussed them with anyone or written them down before. Therefore, they were unthematic. I realize now that a lot of people are probably full of unthematic notions about religion, whether or not they realize it. As for myself, I believe in the idea that the unquestioned faith isn't worth having, and although I may be confused and uncertain I am at least making progress thanks to classes such as this and my own recognition that there is more to life than there appears to be at face value.

Much of the progress I have made in understanding my faith has been through what we have discussed as transcendental experiences, or the ability to reach beyond persons, places, events, etc., ultimately to God or mystery. The idea that every human being has the God-given capability to transcend and, therefore, a chance at salvation has raised some controversy in my mind. Originally I accepted and believed this idea without hesitation, but then images began to flash before me. I envision a hopelessly crippled and retarded person who doesn't even have a mind as we know it, or a starving child in India who doesn't know where his next meal is coming from or if he'll get one. Neither of these people, among many other types, probably even realize their capability to transcend and search for an ultimate meaning in life, nor would they be interested in doing so if they did. Maybe I underestimate these people, or God, but it just seems that some of us have quite an unfair advantage in finding meaning in life.

I feel very fortunate to say that I have transcendental experiences and that I fairly often wonder who I really am and what life is all about. These experiences sometimes get me through the days when I feel nothing is right. Before I took this class I didn't have a name for these experiences or even realize their extent. I don't see how *extremely* unfortunate people can possibly see beyond their suffering and try to find meaning in life or God.

First of all, it would seem that most of them would have so many other worldly pressures and worries upon their shoulders that they wouldn't have time to deal with a search for God. They might be so exhausted from trying to survive in this world that they would have no energy left for other realms. Secondly, if these people did start to transcend their misfortunes I would think they would feel that life is terribly and unnecessarily cruel. They might even be somewhat resentful that they should have to look for some good in their lives. I am not one to believe that God sends us suffering just because he knows we can handle it. What purpose would this serve if He is truly a compassionate God? I do agree, however, with Victor Frankl, author of *Man's Search for Meaning,* that when we are dealt a hardship we must find a basic meaning or something worthwhile to live for in order to cope with the situation. I wish I could understand what it is that makes these unfortunate people I speak of go on. Maybe it is that magnet we speak of, God, which is drawing them out in an especially sensitive way because they are very special people.

Once again, I reach no conclusion. I only sit here in awe, feeling blessed that I have many things in life that help me survive any hardship I am dealt. Somehow I am sure I have overlooked many aspects of this issue and that, very possibly, these people do have their own potential for transcending whether they or I realize it or not. Although I am left with a feeling of helplessness, and at times despair, I have this hope that helps me muddle through all this. It is the hope that some day when I leave this world I *will* understand, and no one can take that hope away.

Within our lifetimes we encounter some experiences that are far beyond the ordinary. It is very possible that some of these will be what we refer to as depth experiences, which we claim to have the three characteristics of being memorable, being a source of decision, and tending to unify our lives. The very first time I heard this definition of a depth experience in class I was taken back by it. I agreed that a depth experience had to be memorable, that seemed very logical. I also agreed that it had to be a source of decision: in other words, it had to make me come to some conclusions which would affect my future actions. However, I very much disagreed that a depth experience necessarily tended to unify my life.

To illustrate my opinion, take the case of a girl who recently got engaged and is deeply in love. All three characteristics of a depth experience as we know it might seem totally in order. Although she might be somewhat scared about the commitment she is making, the declaration of her love for only one man for now and forever is a memorable experience, a source of decision, *and* it tends to unify her life. The case may be the same for another student who receives a long awaited and desperately hoped-for job offer and somehow sees God behind it. For me, however, and I would not be surprised to find this applying to some others, the most important depth experience in my life has done anything *but* unify my life—at least so far.

The depth experience I am speaking of, and which all my other depth experiences seem to be in the shadow of at present, is the recent death of my father. Although definitely memorable and a source of decision, this experience has left me feeling as if my life is in a constant state of disarray. The time following the immediate loss of my father is nothing more than a blur. Days upon days seemed to be spent doing nothing but letting the reality of what had happened sink in, until I was suddenly thrust back into a different kind of reality which demanded my participation in it.

For me, having to get back into the swing of things has only made my life more complicated. Now I am worried about my mother, especially, and my sisters at home. I have schoolwork to think about, deadlines to meet, responsibilities to live up to and all of this is on top of a head full of half-dealt-with questions and many still unasked ones. Values that were once important I am now questioning, as well as things I once thought unimportant. It is as if my life were in the process of a major audit in which I can't decide what to throw out and what to keep, but meanwhile there are also many other worldly things that require my attention and I can't even get around to completing the audit. Every joint that once seemed strong and sturdy now seems to be shaky, faltering.

This is why I say my depth experience has not unified my life, and I can't help but think that someone who has had an experience in any way similar to mine might feel the same. It makes you fall to pieces for a while. For a while—that seems to be the key. Despite everything I have said, I am all right. I'm doing fine. I find the strength every day to go on.

Perhaps it would be better to think of a depth experience as *eventually* unifying our lives. The idea seems much more settling to me this way; because I am fairly confident that once I, and others in similar situations, have had enough time to ask all the questions we want and think all we want, our lives will be more unified because we were forced to take a good hard look at them.

Some other figures and concepts that are often taken for granted, but which really need to be dealt with, are Jesus Christ and the Kingdom of God. I believe God disclosed himself to us most obviously through the human form of Jesus Christ, although He discloses himself every day through things as simple as the trees or a family meal. These disclosures are all part of God's revelation. I don't think I ever truly realized how human Jesus Christ actually was. I always had an image of him as a divine magical spirit that could take the shape of a human, or any other shape for that matter, it wanted to. I still believe that Jesus Christ was divine, but now I realize he was just as much human. I think God made a special case out of Jesus Christ and sent him into our world in human form to show us just how deep a relationship and how much love God offers us.

I believe Jesus Christ was divine, first and foremost, because God brought him into the world as a human *under special circumstances.* Just by this he could not be the same as every other human. His mother was a virgin, he had powers no other human had, he had ultimate knowledge of God, etc. Yet, he was human. Jesus needed to eat and drink, he felt physical pain, he got impatient, he cried. And the characteristics go on and on. Since Jesus was a special case, though, it is my belief that no one presently on this earth has divine capabilities equal to Jesus' or will ever have them on this earth. Some theologians, however, believe that all humans have the same capacity to know God's infinitude as Jesus Christ did. Saying this takes away from the divinity and uniqueness of Jesus for me.

I base my belief that we will not know God's infinitude until after we die on the observation that there has never been another person on this earth who was as completely transcendent or aware of God's infinitude as Jesus. I can't believe that there is not one soul on this earth ready enough or worthy enough for God to reveal his infinitude to. I think there are at least a handful of these people. Although the world is mostly full of average and "bad" people, there are some that are saint-like and very actively seeking out God. Why would God offer such a gift and then not give it to those worthy of it? Rather, I believe that we will only receive this gift from God after we have died. Therefore, we achieve divinity also only after death.

To say that every human has the possibility of becoming the type of divine human Jesus was would seem to provoke the question, "So why the big deal about Jesus Christ?" For me this will never be the case. Jesus Christ was different from any state which humans as I know them can achieve.

The Kingdom of God is a concept still somewhat mysterious to me. I know a little bit more now of what it is not. It is not necessarily heaven, although I am sure the Kingdom of God is present in heaven. Rather, the Kingdom of God was present in the past, is present now, and will be present in the future. For me the Kingdom of God is one of the greatest signs of hope that there truly is a life with God after our physical life, a heaven. This is because the Kingdom of God is based on the belief that human beings left to themselves could never achieve justice, peace, or harmony. Rather they would lead lives seeking selfish self-fulfillment. Obviously though, this is not the case, because in our world there *is* a quest for truth and love. All is not bad.

To sum up, the clearest concept I have of the Kingdom of God is that it is a condition or state, not a place, which is created when God's name is held sacred, a homeless person is sheltered, a lonely person is given companionship, or any other act of love or charity is performed. I think this understanding is quite sufficient for the time being, especially since we know that every time we partake in one of these acts we are helping to actually bring about the Kingdom of God.

There is a quote by the famous theologian, Karl Rahner, which I believe is very thought-provoking and which hours upon hours could be devoted to in order to do it justice. For myself, it seems to compact a great deal of what I have been professing into a single clear, concise sentence and the quote is this: "Every human being spends a lifetime on the shore of the sea of infinite mystery, busy with the grains of sand he or she finds there."

This quote brings to mind an image of my life, and the lives of others, as the shore of a sea. On three vague "sides" I am surrounded by people and things I have experienced in my life such as my family, childhood friends, grade school, high school, teachers, and college community. The list goes on and on. This is the context out of which I have thus far lived my life. Every part of it has touched me or had an influence on me and, therefore, has made me who and what I am today—just as all the soil, sand, sunshine, water, insects, and feet that cross the seashore make it what it is.

Still, beyond these three "sides" and to the fourth "side," the sea itself to which I can find no end, there is even more life for me to experience in the future. There will be more unthematic ideas to become thematic expressions, more people, lands, opportunities, fortunes, hardships, etc., just as the seashore will experience more changes and become eroded, littered, more beautiful, or whatever. These are our horizons, of which we can only be certain about one thing—they will expand. We do not, however, have any idea of what they hold in store for us. Only as they become part of our contexts will we be able to look back and realize that they were once part of our horizons.

When I mentioned the "side" of my context which surrounds me but seems to have no end, I meant to imply that this was the constant search for meaning in my life, seemingly with no definite answer. This search was illustrated in my previous paragraphs as unanswered questions and states of uncertainty.

It struck me, though, as I reread it, that the vast and rough waters of the sea or ocean that people find scary are really strikingly similar to this search for meaning in life. On safe ground we have some knowledge of large bodies of water and do not fear them, but once we embark upon them we can easily be thrown into a frenzy and lose all our good sense about them. I consider a search for meaning in our lives to be a vital necessity. But once we begin we can easily be panicked into thinking that there is no meaning, or else we can become frustrated to find that meaning is not always constant and sometimes changes.

I say lucky are the people who can occasionally take a dip into these waters beyond their contexts, finding even a little more inner peace and insight into why things happen the way they do. They have transcended their normal everyday lives, which I believe people don't often take the time to do, and have gotten more in touch with the meaning, or God, in their lives. They may flow back in with the tide, but at least they won't have to say in their loneliest and most depressed day that they have missed something but can't quite put their finger on what it is.

The states which they and I flow back to are, as I previously mentioned, our normal everyday lives. It is here that I believe the grains of sand come into the picture. Every situation or experience we encounter in an hour, a day, a month, or a year is another grain of sand in a vast beach of which the grains could never be counted. On the same note, we will never be able to keep track of all the experiences which we deal with in our lives and which we are knowingly or unknowingly affected by. Sometimes, though, these experiences are so moving or jarring that we immediately feel they have revealed something to us. The birth of a baby, the power of a raging thunderstorm, or the beauty of the sunset on a seashore may merely be grains of sand; but they can also be tremendous depth experiences by which we become aware of meaning, or God, in a deeper or different sense.

And so there sits my seashore, just as I am sure there is one for every person on this earth. It is evolving constantly, and I along with it. For now I am seated on dry land just dangling my feet in the water—only to become completely submerged after I pass out of this world.

MAUREEN KARNATZ

WHAT is theology and what is it all about? Like the mathematical and philosophical sciences, theology begins with questioning and man's "desire to know." However, it differs from these kinds of sciences in the types of questions it asks. I think that the defining questions of theology are the ones which ask who God is and what he means for us, as humans. These questions result in other questions about who we are and what we mean for the world. Karl Rahner believes the answers to these questions are one and the same: "We can only seek God as we seek true humanity, we can only find truth about ourselves as we find truth about God."

If this is so, I believe that our Christian faith can be defined as our personal knowledge of God gained through our experience of God. Our faith also is, therefore, our ability to let ourselves go, to leave all security behind, and to dive into the infinite mystery of God. By interpreting our faith, then, we can derive our own personal theologies about the meaning of God and the meaning of our human existence. These theologies are the theological anthropologies, because they are studies of the meaning of life for all humanity. We are all concerned about "who we are," and, therefore, are trying to unravel the most familiar mystery of our lives, that of the meaning of our existence as human beings. I believe this common experience all humans share provides a sense of unity within the world and within our evolutionary process of development.

In explaining this mystery of who we are, I like the analogy of a person standing at the edge of an ocean, wiggling his or her toes in the wet sand there. Just as the person looking out over the ocean at the horizon feels as if the horizon goes on forever, we, as humans, in searching for meaning in our lives, realize that there is no finite limit to what we can become. The meaning of our lives is, consequently, a mystery—an ever-expanding horizon.

Without knowing it, we give meaning to our lives through everyday experiences, actions, and thoughts. But we are not aware that we are doing this—it is a sort of unthematic knowledge. We are like the person who is busy with the grains of sand at the edge of the ocean, unaware that he or she is wiggling his or her toes in the wet sand.

In this sense, I think that all of our experiences, both insignificant and significant, have a religious meaning; because, by giving meaning to our lives, they bring us closer to God. I think that this is what religion is all about. It is an awareness of God in one's life as evidenced by a combination of various attitudes, convictions, emotions, rituals, beliefs, and institutions. Through these, we come to terms with and express our most fundamental relationship with reality and the created order as coming from God's creative hand. Thus, there is a religious element in the experiences of every human being, whether or not he or she is conscious of it and whether or not he or she actually believes in God.

Even if we choose to ignore God, I think that religion plays a part in our lives. By denying God, we simply choose to forego "becoming higher" in the history of humanity. But we can always decide to turn around and

accept God again, because he never goes away. Therefore, once we have faith in God as an infinite mystery,
we are giving ultimate meaning to our lives and are becoming part of a "salvation history." In other words,
since all humanity is involved in the ongoing process of a
search for meaning, if we accept God's self-communication, which is present within all history, we will be led
toward both an individual and a world fulfillment of the
meaning of human life.

But how does one get closer to this ultimate meaning
in life, this mystery? Referring back to the horizon
analogy, each of our experiences occurs within a finite
horizon of understanding. As we move beyond every
limited horizon of understanding, or transcend our ordinary concrete tangible experiences, we realize the ever-
receding infinity of the horizon. Hans Küng says that
"nothing is more human than to go beyond that which
is." Therefore, in order to find meaning in life, man
must transcend himself. He accomplishes this both
through everyday experiences and depth experiences.

During this experience of self-transcendence, there is
also a certain immanence to our being. We must realize
that we can only come out of ourselves if a part of ourselves remains immobile, attesting to the fact that mere
existence presumes a meaning in life. Thus, secularization is a force present within our lives, for we are not
seeking the answer to the meaning of our existence from
the church, but rather from the realities in our everyday
lives. I think this means that in our search for truth and
love, we tend to move away from an extrinsic authority's determination of these values and favor the authority of our own personal reasoning.

This way of thinking is the product of the Enlightenment of the seventeenth and eighteenth centuries. This period was one of great crisis in the church, which faced a turning point in its existence because not all of its people accepted its determination of truth any longer. Rather, people wanted to reason for themselves what the truth in life was and how they could give ultimate meaning to their lives. Therefore, we have moved away from what the church says is reality and have tried to arrive at the answers within our world itself, or within our *weltanschauung*.

As a result, some theologians today believe that the only finite limit to the meaning of our lives is an infinite mystery, or God. That is, "God is the meaning of who we are." I think that our desire to understand and to pose questions about this mystery indicates our belief that the mystery actually does exist. I also think that our human ability to come to know this infinite mystery as the meaning of our lives is best represented through the person of Jesus Christ, the perfect human being.

Jesus Christ came to know God gradually, by continually transcending himself in order to completely accept God's "self-gift." God's self-gift is His self-communication; or, as Rahner says, God, "the giver, is Himself the gift." This self-communication of God is also known as grace. God's grace penetrates into every sphere of our lives, thus making human existence a graced existence.

We, as humans, have the capacity to reject or accept grace in every experience of our lives. Jesus, as a human, totally accepted God's self-gift and thus became divine while also remaining human to an extent which we can

never hope to match. I think this is because we sometimes become alienated from ourselves and reject God's
self-gift. But by understanding that Jesus, as a human,
in his search for ultimate meaning, totally accepted
God's self-gift, I think that we can at least realize that
we also have the potential to do the same.

I think it is obvious that I am in favor of an historical
approach in forming a personal theology. An historical
approach can also be referred to as a "Christology from
below." This expression indicates that my theology, like
Karl Rahner's, begins with Jesus as a man in history
and, by considering the events of his life, comes to an
understanding of him as Rahner's "Christ of God."

I think that understanding a Christology from below
is difficult for many people because we are so used to accepting the words of the Bible as literal interpretations
of what occurred during Jesus' life. In fact, it was not
until 1943 that Pope Pius XII said that theologians
could use historical methods to assess the levels of tradition in the Bible. These levels of tradition consist of
three stages. The first stage is that of the original words
of Jesus Christ. The second stage consists of the oral
proclamations or stories about Jesus' words. And the
final stage is that of the actual writings of the evangelists
themselves. The historical method which theologians
used to interpret the Bible in 1943 is the basis for today's
Christology from below.

But how can we, as Christians, interpret the Bible's
message for us today? By demythologizing the Bible—
that is, by translating its message from the terms of the
situation and the mythological world picture of that
time into the terms of our situation and the modern

world picture of today—we begin to understand the meaning of Christ's existence as it pertains to us today. Therefore, I think a Christology from below is a realistic approach to theology, because it gives a sense of dignity to man as he realizes that Jesus, as a man, was a human being with qualities similar to those of human beings today.

One of the most common concepts in the Bible that is now demythologized is that of the Kingdom of God. The Kingdom of God can only be expressed by metaphors like the mustard seed in the Bible. We demythologize this parable and arrive at an understanding of the Kingdom of God as both a process and a reality toward which we are moving. It is a condition which is not only in the future, but is also in the past and the present. I think this portrayal of the Kingdom of God is hard to accept for many people who believe there is a final and predetermined destiny in their lives. Their idea of the Kingdom of God as an actual place offers them a sense of security and reward for having been loving, generous, and loyal worshipers of God. But I think that the view of the Kingdom of God as an ongoing process gives man more of a sense of responsibility, because he is now becoming what he is eventually going to be. Therefore, I believe that man co-creates the Kingdom of God.

In the Bible there is an apocalyptic genre that describes the "last" things in life, such as the Kingdom of God, heaven, hell, and judgment. The emphasis of this style of writing is on visions, signs, and predictions of future events brought about entirely by divine power. I think that this way of expressing eschatology, or the study of the last things in life, makes the day of our death seem final and the rest of our life trivial. By simply demythologizing this apocalyptic writing, though, I think we see that where we end up at the end of life is largely due to the decisions we make as to how to behave and what to think during our lives. Our day-to-day existence is more worthwhile and significant when we describe the Kingdom of God in this fashion. Moreover, to make a mistake, to sin, is only to get tripped up in our search for what life is all about. Consequently, our faith in God as the meaning of who we are becomes what we live. Our search for the meaning of our lives is our effort to create the Kingdom of God through our love of God and our neighbors.

The miracles in the Bible can also be demythologized to help us look at the importance of Jesus in a new way. I think that, for the most part, miracles were designed to explain certain occurrences in a culture in which the people did not know how to explain them in any other manner. Once demythologized, though, the miracles show that Jesus was a man of tremendous power; and they indicate what the Kingdom of God, in its most perfect form, consists of. I also believe the miracles testify to Jesus' power over life and death, along with his overwhelming compassion for mankind. Finally, I think miracles have a lot to do with our initiation into the Christian faith, because their fantastic qualities make the man Jesus seem all the more a perfect model for us to imitate in our search for the meaning of life.

So where does the church fit into all of this? I believe that the role of the church is to show people that we, as Christians, really believe that God is in our midst. It is also to proclaim the Word of God to the world and to serve the world's people, no matter what religion they belong to. But where does the Church get its dogma and rules from? These are simply the products of revelation. God reveals or communicates himself through creation, events, persons, and especially Jesus. In this way, although His message is mysterious, we come to know God and how He wants us to live.

But what is God's message and his will for us, anyway? In essence, God is concerned with man's cause, man's well-being. God's will is the humanization of man, or the process by which we and our history come closer to our final destiny in God. God, I think, wants each man to be the best human being he can be. In other words, He wants man never to stop accepting his grace and to continually search for the meaning of life. He does not want man to merely exist as a human being, as a "blob of matter," but to *be* human by gradually discovering the role of God in his life. Jesus, as a human being, also served this cause in the world.

However, in being human, man must frequently choose what direction to take. Despite certain determining factors in our lives—such as our birth, our physical and psychic makeup, our historical and cultural situation, our limited intellectual and emotional capacity, our past decisions, our unavoidable death, and others— we have the transcendental ability to make choices which will determine our development as human beings. The decisions we make, both conscious and unconscious ones, affect our existence and, consequently, the meaning of who we are. Even in the case of conversion, the convert is engaged in an ongoing process of discovering the meaning of who he or she is.

Jesus wanted people to convert because he wanted people to make a decision, to face a turning point at which their lives could go either in the direction of saying "yes" to God or that of saying "no" to God. Obviously, he wanted people to say "yes" to God by acting in the interests of others instead of in their own interests.

This concept of conversion is similar to Karl Rahner's concept of the fundamental option. The fundamental option is one's decision for or against God. We have the freedom to choose to say either "yes" or "no." By saying "yes," we admit that there is something more to our existence than merely an array of biological, sociological, and psychological determining factors. Therefore, our freedom is our ability to be someone, to unconsciously transcend ourselves, and to get to know God. Most important, opting freely for God guarantees that all our actions and experiences will derive their meaning in the light of God's will, our humanization.

But what happens if we reject God, if we do not accept His self-gift? I believe that we can never be fully sure that we have definitely said "no" to God. Even if all our acts are done selfishly, and we are unable to experience truth and love, I think we still give meaning to our lives. But this is not a meaning which allows us to "become higher." Sinful acts force the history of salvation and the evolution of man to slow down because, by committing them, we are not striving to become more fully actualized—that is, more perfect human beings. We are simply refusing to discover that our lives have their ultimate meaning in God, in His boundless compassion, love, and generosity. Therefore, the choice of saying either "yes" or "no" to God makes man unique, or different from all of God's other creations. Man is unrestrained in his ongoing process of deciding which direction to take in life.

Consequently, we see that the meaning of our lives depends on whether we answer or refuse to answer to God. The question of "who we are" is revealed to us through God's self-communication, as is its answer. This search for the meaning of our lives is an ongoing endeavor and is always subject to change.

I was once asked if I thought that we, as humans, are passing through time or that time is passing through us. I believe that we are passing through time; because our existence, our quest for meaning, has an end beyond itself—to further the development of the history of salvation. If time passed through us, we would play no real role in evolution. We would simply be matter acted upon by external forces. However, I think we are active in time. Our freely made decisions are what allow us to transcend the many given factors which we have no control over in our lives and, within and throughout all time, to give ultimate meaning to life.

Therefore, in conclusion, I think that giving meaning to life is the purpose of the existence of humanity. By wholeheartedly saying "yes" to the search for meaning, and thus to God, we profess faith in God. This faith allows us to prepare to sacrifice everything for our God and to trust in his power over evil. This faith also both gives us hope and courage to face the future and provides a basis for our world community to share in mutual respect and love. Since all humanity shares the common experience of the need to give meaning to life, would it not be wonderful if people from all nations could have faith in the infinite mystery of God as the answer to their search?

Thus the question of who God is and what he means for us as humans arises again. Because I believe this is the defining question of theology, I have tried to answer it in my attempt at a personal theology. And I will always be trying to answer it throughout my life as I continually decide, as a Christian, to say "yes" to God through my actions, thoughts and experiences.

ANNE MONASTYRSKI

FAITH hinges on two questions: "Who am I?" and "What is the meaning of it all?" If both questions were a matter of accumulating knowledge which could be fully grasped at a certain point in my life, there would be no need for religious beliefs. Faith would be a matter of choice, and at the same time it would be no faith at all since it would be based on fact. But faith exists because man cannot know everything and yet believes nonetheless.

But to understand faith and to understand what I believe and why I believe it, I must question. In fact, I cannot claim a faith until I have questioned; so central is questioning to faith, which is a quest. And so I begin at the most basic question, which ironically is also unanswerable at any point during my life: "Who am I?" Jesus himself wrestled with this. In his struggle to learn who he was it becomes easier to see his humanness. I do not expect to be able to say at any point in my lifetime, "This is who I am." My life, taken experience by experience, becomes pieces of the whole of who I am. Each experience helps me to reach even deeper in my self until, ultimately, I discover who I am at the end of my life.

Experience is that which teaches me about myself and my relationship to others. Each experience, each accomplishment, spurs me on to yet another; no one goal that is reached will satisfy me. Humans are always capable of doing more. Humans have limited mental and physical capacities, but in our capacity to love and give of our-

71

selves to one another the horizon of capacity moves ever onward into the infinite.

It is my ability to love which reveals to me the human capacity of transcendence and immanence. Once I recognize that my parameters are set—and they are set at the Infinite—then I am ready to journey towards the Kingdom where the journey ends, when I reach Reality.

And so, experience by experience, I continue to grope through the blindness to who I am while I reach out to others as guideposts along the way. For it is in relating to and with others that I gradually learn more about who I am. But it is more than just "people." It is when I see people as ever larger communities that I begin to see others as also journeying toward the Kingdom: from a circle of family members to the larger circle of friends, the larger circle of peers and acquaintances, and on. My relationship to others has a rippling effect. Thus it is possible to see myself as related to the "people" all over the world who remain nameless faces. There is a continuity of community among us. The rippling effect also explains my responsibilities towards others. While the direct impact of my actions is most easily recognized within the circles closest to me, my actions nevertheless do ripple outward. Because of this, I cannot agree with those who think their individual actions have no implication world-wide.

While I am constantly reaching out to others and simultaneously reaching into myself to learn more of who I am, I do not lose my identity or become less of a person. In fact, in giving of myself I am realizing more of my potential as a transcendent and immanent being. Coupled with this experience is my more cosmic experience of knowing that no one accomplishment is totally satisfying. Every goal becomes a new challenge to do better, do more, reach further.

Because I sense these two qualities, I believe there is something more to life than just life itself, something that gives meaning to life, to the few and meagre days I spend on earth. It is Reality. Reality calls me to be in touch with life as it is, not as I would wish it to be. The closer I am to accepting reality and the more I strive to deal with reality, the closer I grow toward becoming one with Reality.

Taken this way, life is not a series of trials where we are tested and if we pass the test we go to heaven. Life is a growing experience whereby, through others, and through a personal relationship with Reality, we travel closer to Reality. Death becomes an experience through which we grow closer to Reality. It is one *real* event we all share, among the other disillusioning events of life. It is part of the process of the journey to be united with Reality, when we become fully human. People's unwillingness to accept Reality frustrates them, so they continue to seek God in the abstract, in the "heavens," in their imaginations. Accepting reality means living through and for others, since Reality is in each of these persons, who, like me, are capable of transcendence and immanence.

It is easier for me to comprehend God in terms of Reality than in those forms which end up gendering God. Using "God" does not bother me unless God becomes a he or a she.

I believe we can have a personal relationship with Reality. Reality is not an external force acting upon my life. I can know Reality because Reality wills to be revealed to humans. Reality works through time and history, through persons, events, creation; and in my openness to these things, Reality becomes personally involved in my life and is revealed more and more.

Although I have felt this presence in my life and through historical events, I have never attached a word to it. And before this course, "grace" was just an ethereal word. Now I have come to put the idea and word together. Karl Rahner's interpretation of and outlook on the meaning of grace brings a new dimension to grace in my life; it is no longer part of the supernatural. Reality is present during every moment of my life regardless of whether or not I am conscious of it.

What is more important is the realization that Reality is present in others; and so it is through other humans, once again, that I reach out to Reality and Reality draws me. The beauty of grace is that it is something offered to me; it is a gift. Within my personal relationship with Reality, Reality calls me to see Reality in others, to grow closer to others, and thereby grow closer to Reality. Reality is present through all of this through grace.

Grace is always here for us, but we are not always receptive to the presence of Reality. There is a tension which exists, in that we have a propensity toward Reality yet have a tendency to block out grace from coming into our lives. It is during these times that we sometimes allow evil to affect us. I believe evil exists and that sometimes we inflict evil on others, deliberately or unwittingly.

But I do not dwell on the idea of sin, because it prevents me even further from growing in my relationship with Reality and only creates bigger blocks between grace and me. There is a tendency, however, to explain evil as an external force which causes people to do bad things to other people. Just as I believe that people have a great potential within them which remains latent until they grow in faith to be able to use the power, so I believe that people have the potential within them to bring about evil. It is part of the imperfect nature of humans.

The evils of loneliness, sickness, pain and lack of freedom still puzzle me. In some sense I can reconcile these with my faith. But there is much that I cannot fully understand and believe with true conviction. I believe all are invited to journey toward the Kingdom, to be co-builders. This implies freedom to choose this path. Schizophrenics seem to lack an ability to deal with reality; it is as if they completely block off grace from their lives. I cannot say, however, that this is a choice, for they seem to search for freedom yet cannot find the path toward reality. This is an evil of which they are the victims; and while I can accept the fact that there is a purpose in the overall plan of moving toward the Kingdom that some people should be sick, I cannot reconcile this with the idea of free will.

I cannot be satisfied with the idea that just because I cannot reconcile it, the evil must be "God's will." In many instances this amounts to throwing one's hands up and leaving the explanation at that. Many think that dying is evil, but death is part of the process of growing towards our eventual union with Reality. Thus, death has meaning. Although it is painful to lose someone I love, it is not an emptying experience nor an empty experience. That person is still part of my life. If, in death, a person is united with Reality, and Reality is what we strive for, and Reality is transcendent and immanent, then that person must still be human in his capacity to do this. If death is not the end, then it cannot be evil. God wills that we all someday reach the Kingdom through our growing realization of what it means to be human. God wills that we realize our human potential to bring about the Kingdom.

It is in this part of my faith that Jesus Christ enters. I understand Jesus from two perspectives. With God as a reference point, Jesus is the ultimate form of grace and revelation. Jesus was so in touch with Reality that he became Reality. In him and through him I see Reality. From the human perspective, Jesus was a person who gradually, through experience, came to know Reality. Since Jesus was totally open to grace he became the ultimate form of transcendence and immanence; he realized in his life what it means to become fully human. In this, Jesus is divine.

A crucial part of my faith rests in my belief that Jesus was fully divine and fully human. His humanity must not be slighted. What Jesus worked for during his entire life cannot have meaning for me if I am told to believe the he was God and man without fully understanding the human side of him, that quintessence of humanity which makes his life relevant to mine. Like all of us, Jesus struggled with himself to try to discover who he was. He had to have come to a gradual realization that he was called to do great things in his life—just as we all are—but that he also grew in understanding that he was in touch with Reality, fully.

Too many of our lessons on the life of Jesus are spent emphasizing the divine part of him at the expense of his humanity, and yet we are taught to strive to live in the same way. Frustrating as it is, we end up trying to follow the example of a being, who, because he was also God, had it made. His life becomes a farce, but we are nevertheless told to role play. And we necessarily fail, since, unlike Jesus, we lack the divine "half" of ourselves.

Jesus, wholly human and wholly divine, becomes a hope and a promise for the day we will reach our potential to bring about the Kingdom. To live a life like that of Jesus becomes a goal on the horizon at the point where the horizon finally rests.

It is not sufficient to discuss the nature of Jesus without discussing his message at the same time. Jesus lived his message, he did not simply preach. In this respect he reveals the social responsibility inherent in living a life of Christ. We are all co-workers building the Kingdom; we cannot do it alone. Part of Jesus' living out his message through his action is witnessed in his miracles. Miracles are an important part of my faith in Jesus because they show the latent power of faith in humans. They are attributes of the power which comes through being completely in touch with Reality. Because Jesus was so locked into what Reality is, he fulfilled the potential all humans have. It was important to Jesus' message that he work miracles, since he always lived out his convictions. Through miracles Jesus touched other persons with his vision of Reality.

I believe that when Jesus was dying he, like all of us, wondered what was the purpose and meaning of it all. Why bother to live a life according to one's own convic-

tions, to share a dream which one believes to be a reality
with one's closest friends, only to be abandoned and feel
utterly devastated when the crucial moment arrives and
one is left to die alone? The view of life becomes
nihilistic except for the fact of the resurrection. Without
the faith in a new life after death, death would be the
end; and life with all its injustice and inequity would
have no meaning.

It is not important to me whether Jesus arose in his
human body. What is important is the leap of faith
which is involved if we accept the resurrection. For in
the resurrection lies the infinite; it releases us from the
boundaries of what can be known, and heads us towards
that which cannot be defined but which holds the promise of eternity.

The resurrection, then, becomes the focal point of my
faith in Jesus, in my faith in the purpose and meaning of
life. Jesus' resurrection defines the purpose in life. For
the resurrection to have meaning in my life, I must,
however, internalize it, so that it becomes real for me. I
must experience the resurrection in my life.

Easter Sunday can no longer merely be the commem-
oration of an event, as it was when I was a child. It
becomes a real challenge in my life. It challenges how I
live. Faith in the resurrection means no fear of death.
Living one day at a time is a central part of my philosophy of life. I cannot know the future; therefore I
cannot waste one precious day in anxiety over things
which I, as a human, have no power to control. But
faith in the resurrection also challenges me to put myself
totally off my guard and defenseless, trusting that Reality will always be there for me. By total trusting, I

become vulnerable because I no longer wrap my limitations around me to protect me in my insecurities. But also, in total trust in Reality and the faith of the resurrection, I open myself up to all the power of Reality, to work through me so that I can be the best possible co-builder of the Kingdom. What a gift this is, just waiting for us to reach for it.

Though time passes and I grow in and through future experiences, I do not believe these bases of my faith should ever change. For I am at rock bottom and must build on from here with the help of others and Reality.

PATRICK BARRY

TO arrive at one's true beliefs is a very difficult task, since there is such a striking contrast between all the previous teachings that we have been told to believe and our knowledge of how the world is actually being run. I don't imagine it is ever easy to arrive at what one really believes about who he is and why he is here, but I think it is essential that we constantly and continually make the effort. This responsibility is especially difficult for today's generation because we are more aware of the diversities and the complications in the world than any previous generation has been.

We have been raised by people who learned life from the teachings of our grandparents, which were primarily based on their experiences. Our parents learned religion and life's fundamentals because they were "told to," and they subsequently drew upon their parents' good judgment and rigid theological upbringing to understand their own experiences and used those same methods in raising us. But we also had a new and completely different learning source: television. We know more about the world, its vast differences and its mindboggling complexity, and are forced to face the problems of life's confusion at a very early age. We were made aware of many different beliefs and religions, and we asked why ours was necessarily THE one true religion. The "I told you something, so believe it" attitude was being challenged, and questions needed to be answered. They still do.

Our generation is now searching for those answers; and although some of the older generation may think that we lack faith, I think that our search will provide the foundation for a very strong faith that we can believe in and live with. It will be a stronger conviction because we are forced to make a stand and believe in something because it is right for us and not because we were told to believe it.

Unfortunately, the challenge of the traditional way of teaching theological doctrine has brought about a wave of apathy and irresponsible attitudes. I think that we should be encouraged not only to ask questions and seek answers, but especially to form a judgment based on logic and well thought out arguments. An attitude of "Well, you have one opinion and I have another; and since we will never be able to prove either argument, to each his own" is not only a very irresponsible argument but also a very dangerous one.

There must be some measuring stick to compare different viewpoints, and I think that standard should be the logic and the fundamental priorities that the argument depends on. For instance I think it would generally be agreed that a method for conducting one's life that centers around others is a more fundamentally sound method than one that centers around money or materialistic objects. All people should address the problem, discuss it, challenge each other and themselves, and form a set of values that will lay down the basis for a very strong, logically based faith.

But the question still remains of how we are to come to an understanding of what we are doing here and who we are. Before I attack the problem of who I am, I think it is important to realize my limitations and my inability to understand many abstract concepts. Being human, I realize that I am restricted to my own experiences and those of others, each colored by biases and prejudices, as well as being restricted by the physical boundaries of the world around me. I have to realize that I will never obtain all the answers or prove anything definitely, but it is important to constantly try to get closer to an ultimate meaning in my life.

I have found a good starting point for this search to be myself. This is not a selfish start but one that is reasonable, since it is my life that I am trying to make sense of. I form a set of values and list them in order of priority to determine what should be the most important thing in my life. It is important to note the distinction between what is important to me and what should be important to me, since I don't necessarily want to rank those things that I would actually choose as more valuable but rather those things that I *should* choose. This way I am able to arrive at sound guidelines from which I can always compare my existing values and thus always be aiming to strengthen my value system.

For instance I value myself a great deal. I take care of myself and go to great lengths to provide comfort to myself. Now I ask myself if there is anything that I should give up my life for. The answer is that I would like to think I would give up my life for the safety of my family and close friends and as well for certain causes. These things I value more than I value my own life. Now I ask myself what do I value more than family or friends. The answer would have to be a principle or set of ideals, since I could think of instances where I would place principles ahead of the lives of my family and friends. This type of hypothetical questioning and answering continues until I arrive at an order of priorities.

At the top of this list would be principles or ideals that would basically be a synopsis of the ten commandments. The emphasis of these ideals would be upon the basic value of all human life. It is this priority system that I would look to for a method of analyzing the moral problems that I face. The fact that a set of principles is at the top of my priority list signifies that I am ultimately accountable for my actions to someone or something.

The priority that I have given the general guidelines that top my list must also be accompanied by a certain authority. In other words, if I place myself at the top of my importance list, then I must answer to myself and justify my actions only to myself. Likewise if I place my family and friends at the top of the list, then my actions must be in harmony with their importance. I could not place my self-interest in front of theirs without having to honestly admit that I was wrong in doing that. The same argument holds for a principle or set of ideals. I cannot place anything ahead of those principles without having to admit that I was wrong in doing so. I should be held accountable for my actions to someone or something other than myself, because I am not as important as some other things in my life.

It is here that I introduce the theological problem of God. First of all, I want to look at what I mean by God. Part of my answer will include that thing or being which I must be accountable to. The things that are most important in my life are incorporated into my definition of God. However there is much more to the idea of God.

I think a good starting place would be to describe God as incomprehensible, unimaginable, and vast beyond all imagination. I think Karl Rahner describes the concept

of God particularly well when he says that God is a
source of mystery, a power, a creator, a source of meaning to everything, and much more.

In trying to understand incomprehensible concepts, it
is a common practice to draw analogies so that the concept can be understood on our level. There is a story I
remember that has a point which can be related to God's
domain. The story was of a young girl writing a letter to
a large eastern newspaper, asking if there was really a
Santa Claus. The editors had somewhat of a dilemma on
their hands, since they had a responsibility for reporting
fact and yet did not want to be blamed for breaking the
hearts of little children everywhere. After much thinking
they responded, "Yes, Virginia, there is a Santa Claus."
Their answer was not merely an appeasement of a little
girl, but also an honest answer. Their reasoning was that
in the spirit of giving, in the expression of genuine care,
and in the unusual social concern for others, there was a
very special spirit or feeling or mystery that was exactly
the idea and essence of Santa Claus.

Perhaps this is just a simple little story, but in it I find
a hint of the type of thing God must incorporate. On a
certain level, I think those editors were right when they
answered that it is in the hearts of people that we all get
a glimpse of something that is very beautiful, and yet the
spirit is not physically there at all. All we feel is a type of
confusing mystery that we don't understand, and yet we
don't have to understand it to appreciate it. I think a
very simple analogy can be made that God must incorporate this idea of a spirit that is in people: beautiful, incomprehensible, and yet if we are willing to look for it,
it is certainly there. The fact that honest, truth-seeking

editors recognized the fact that powers of mystery, hints of meaning, and feelings of genuine caring love do exist made me think that this same type of thing may be extrapolated many times over and would be the type of mystery that God would encompass.

I think the analogy of God's drawing us to him like a magnetic force is an excellent one. The fact that man has always looked for an answer to "Who am I?" and has always looked beyond his own physical surroundings to a mystery indicates to me that man is born with a probing and searching mind as well as with a hint about the source of this mystery.

The methods that we use to try to understand the relationship between ourselves and this God are different, but I think that a good way to try to understand this very special relationship is to draw from various sources. One source is our parents' and other good friends' beliefs, although we must take into account the fact that they have come up with their own understanding of the relationship. From my parents I have a faith in something that is beyond and above me that I have to answer to. This faith is quite strong, but I do not have enough answers to fully substantiate my faith. This faith is based primarily on the experiences of my parents and the realization that they have come to their own understanding of their relationship with God. Where these beliefs came from and under what circumstances these people came to know their faith must be kept in mind.

One problem I have found when trying to understand another's viewpoint is that I have found a lot of "buzz words" that don't mean very much to me. I think it would be very easy to simply say, "If you want to go to heaven then believe in Christ, the Lord your Savior, the son of God. If you don't have faith then your soul will go to hell. I don't know what the problem is, since the Bible says it all right there." Although this kind of explanation is a very fulfilling one to many people whose faith is strong and sincere, I think people often may spew out this sort of rhetoric without understanding what they are talking about. These types of answers are very convenient ones, but they are not prepackaged panaceas for life. This rhetoric doesn't mean very much to me, and so an explanation of another's faith using these concepts doesn't have an influence on me.

The idea of my soul's spending the rest of eternity in heaven doesn't exuberantly excite me, nor does the threat that I will rot in hell with the devil bother me. I don't really understand exactly what people are talking about when they say such things. Traditional doctrine and fundamentalist-type explanations do not help me because I don't know what it is that is being said. I do not think that I should disregard what these people say; but instead I should study where these explanations came from, who said them and in what context, and what is the essence of the message. What I do not want to do is to turn to these popular answers and lean on them without being convinced that what I am saying has significant meaning for me.

Another source to consider in my evaluation is a group of men who had tremendous faith and wrote different works that are assembled in a book called the Bible. These works must be viewed with some responsibility so that the point that the authors were trying to make is not lost in the translation. From what little I have studied in the Bible, specifically the New Testament, I have a basic belief in the life and works of Jesus. This belief is still in the developmental and evaluative stage, but I do believe that this man was a very special man. By the way that he lived his life and from what he taught, I realize that this man contributes in a significant way to my relationship with God. Whether this man was the son of God, or born of a virgin, or rose from the dead, are just a few of the questions that I have yet to answer. But I am glad that I have these questions and am not just blindly accepting things.

I think that the proper way to look for these answers is to use a method called historical criticism. This scientific approach looks at the writings of the Bible and analyzes who wrote the text, in what set of circumstances and to whom the text was written, and what the central message is. These analysts look at the original languages and compare and contrast different interpretations in order to arrive at the most accurate interpretation. I think this is a very valuable method to discover what were the messages of the writings of the Bible. From this method I have discovered many items that have given me more faith in the writings of the New Testament and made me a more responsible reader and listener of the "Word of God." I personally place little value in the strict literal sense of the Bible and believe that it is essential to first analyze the text. It is by this method that many questions have been brought to my attention, and it is by this method that I hope to arrive at many answers.

A third source that I think I should draw from is my own experiences. These include everything from my theology class to coping with the death of a family member to watching in awe the beauty of a sunset. These experiences all add another dimension to the relationship of God and myself, and the relationship must account for all these experiences. It is from my personal experiences that I have again discovered many answers as well as many questions. I can't help but think that there is meaning in everything and a power behind it all when I look at a beautiful sky and feel the force of nature around me. I am necessarily led to believe that there is order in all the beautiful complexities of life and that some inconceivable power must be responsible for it.

It is also from my personal experiences that I have come to disagree with the attitude of some people who treat God as though He were simply a very powerful person. When someone close to me dies it is natural to ask, "Why did God take this person away?" But to question God like a school kid seems ridiculous. Why not ask, "Why was I so fortunate that I was allowed to spend so much time with this great person?" In the confusion and complexity of life there are many unanswerable questions, because this is the nature and the essence of life. To reduce the idea of God to the power that decides who dies and who lives on a day-to-day basis is absurd. There must be something more to God than this simple attitude would have us believe.

These sources have also given me a basis to form an opinion on many other fundamental issues that all tie in with my understanding of my relationship with God. With respect to the Catholic Church, I don't believe it is the one and only way for people to discover their purpose here. I think it has been a great foundation and an excellent guideline for many people. I think specifically that it is very meaningful to my parents and has aided them in coming to terms with their relationship to God. However, I really don't know enough about the foundations of the beliefs of the Catholic Church to make an honest appraisal. I have used many of the concepts and beliefs as I know them to base my general faith in God, and I express that faith through the medium of the church, but my knowledge of it is really rather limited.

After all the reflection and review, it is difficult to see exactly what I believe. I am like everyone else in that I am still forming the basis of my faith and still wrestling with many fundamental problems. The key to discovery and to a strong faith is questioning. So long as I always ask questions and seek answers, I think that I will grow in my faith. To summarize my basic beliefs I will rewrite the Apostles' Creed, substituting my convictions for the traditional phrasing.

Apostles' Creed

I believe in God, the Father almighty, creator of heaven and earth; and in Jesus Christ, his only Son our Lord; who was conceived by the Holy Spirit, born of the Virgin Mary, suffered under Pontius Pilate, was crucified, died and was buried. He descended into hell; the third day he rose again from the dead; he ascended into heaven, sits at the right hand of God, the Father almighty; from thence he shall come to judge the living and the dead. I believe in the Holy Spirit, the Holy Catholic Church, the communion of saints, the forgiveness of sins, the resurrection of the body, and life everlasting. Amen.

What I Believe

I do believe in a God. I believe that there is some ultimate meaning and order in life. I think that in everyday experiences we can see the hint of this infinite power and mystery. I think there is a force drawing us out to question and search; this search starts with ourselves and ends with ourselves but encompasses all else in between. This God is responsible for everything that is created in the universe and beyond.

I believe that a great man named Jesus lived and died for a very special cause. I am open to the idea that he was both human and divine but I am still grappling with this idea. I think the best approach to this problem is that of Rahner, who says that Jesus was simply the most complete human and thereby knew exactly who he was and why he was on earth. At the very least I think Jesus was a great man whose life and teachings should be closely examined using the historical critical method. From my personal view I think I should do more studying before I can say that I am very comfortable with this one man's being both divine and human.

I haven't given much theological thought to how Jesus was conceived or born, but it really is not a fundamental element in my theology. I do think that many traditional theologians have had trouble identifying the entrances and exits of Jesus from this world, but at this time I am not fundamentally concerned with it.

I believe he was put to death by crucifixion under Roman rule and supervision.

I believe that Jesus died and that an integral part of him (his soul) went wherever souls go after a human dies. On the third day after Jesus' death, his good friends and disciples came to some very real understanding of what Jesus was doing when he was alive and what his message was. This revelation of the essence of Jesus is vital to the mission of Jesus. I think the explanation whereby Jesus' resurrection is not corporeal and that there is no way to prove anything makes sense. If the secret of Jesus were made fact, then there would be no need for the faith which is an essential part of man's understanding of his relationship with God.

If Jesus was wholly divine and wholly human, then when he died he somehow joined the source of all meaning and mystery. Obviously this concept is beyond my comprehension, but I will admit that it could be that way. It would make sense that we are all here for a reason and that there must be some sort of judgment if we are to exist after we die; therefore that which is the source of all meaning would be a judge. Although I do have problems with this explanation, there probably should be some sort of judging involved.

I do believe in a "holy spirit" in which the source of mystery and the intrinsic urge to seek something that is beyond us is included. We are such complex creatures that the term "holy spirit" also encompasses the power that we can create when we have faith in ourselves and in others.

I believe that the Catholic Church has analyzed the question of "Why are we here?" for years and has some very good explanations. I don't think that it has any absolute answers, but I think the Catholic Church is an excellent place to start looking for some answers to some difficult questions.

I believe there have been many extraordinary humans

who have done incredible things because of their faith and that we should all try to learn from their lives.

I believe that all humans, by the mere fact of being human, are likely to make mistakes, but that there are purposes for those mistakes that only the source of meaning knows. These mistakes are understandable and forgiveable provided that we are sorry for them and try to learn something about ourselves from them.

I haven't decided what the resurrection of the body means, since I just recently discovered that the church has never taught corporeal resurrection.

I believe in some kind of afterlife where the soul continues to exist in one form or another. Since I think that there is some meaning for our existence, I think that this meaning supersedes our physical life and therefore that there must be something after our physical body dies.

Amen.

A STUDENT

WHEN asked to write a paper reflecting my own theology, I initially thought that it would be a fairly easy task. I stopped thinking that once I sat down to ponder what I would put in my paper. What actually is my own theology? Is it what I learned in my religion classes since grade school? Is it what I learn at church? Is it what my parents have taught me?

The theology presented in this paper is not the result of one night's work. I have been formulating it for a while, but never before have I actually written it down or tried to tie all the pieces together so that I could explain it to other people, or to myself. In order to maintain some form of consistency and order, I will try to relate my theology to concepts we have discussed in class rather than going off in a thousand different lines of thought.

Before I could even begin to start writing, I had to answer the above questions and many more. Some of the questions I posed to myself called into question some of the most basic beliefs of Christianity and Catholicism. Some of the answers I found myself giving were quite startling to someone accustomed to simply regurgitating the standard lines that are thrown at him for his entire life.

The questions I have been pondering and seeking to answer for myself are pretty much summed up by Fr. Edward Braxton in his article "A Catholic at Harvard." They are: Is it reasonable to believe in a God as that concept has traditionally been understood? Is Jesus the absolute and unique disclosure of the reality of God? Is

Jesus' "incarnation" any different from the Buddhist
"enlightenment"? If Jesus is unique, is the Roman
Catholic Church alone the authentic continuation of
this historical institution? Is it reasonable to conclude
that the church is capable of providing certain answers
to questions on ethics and other matters?

These basic questions lead to numerous others, but
more importantly they led to a more critical look at what
my theology is and what it stands for. I no longer follow
Catholicism blindly. I have started to think for myself
and often my conclusions are not in accordance with the
Catholic church. This does not mean that I reject
Catholicism; rather it means that I think the Catholic
church's position is not necessarily the one and only correct position on an issue. I think it is very important for
a mature adult to critically evaluate his theology and
then re-affirm it periodically.

I think Dietrich Bonhoeffer, quoted from "The
Changing Forms of Faith," put it well when he stated:

> to entrench ourselves persistently behind the
> 'faith of the Church' is a way of evading the
> honest question as to what we ourselves really
> believe. To hold that the content of faith is the
> Church's business, not that of the individual
> believer, is to shuffle off the responsibility of
> one's faith onto an impersonal institution and
> thus to risk falling into insincerity.

I have been doing a lot of thinking about my Catholic
religion and about the concept of God in general. I have

gradually lost the strength of my childhood faith as I have gotten older and have questioned the beliefs which I so blindly followed as a child. Questioning and finding serious doubts about such an important subject creates a tremendous amount of confusion and uncertainty. This class has added much fuel to the fire of my thoughts and seems in some ways to confirm a few of my doubts.

I believe that there is in all likelihood some sort of Ultimate Reality in the universe. I am not sure that the Catholic version of God is the sole correct way of attempting to unravel the mystery of God. I find it extremely difficult to believe that the Moslem, the Hindu, or the Baptist is not finding and worshipping the same God as we Catholics do, or some other real God; I can not believe that they are just indulging in exercises of futility. I can not believe and do not accept the claim that Catholics or Christians are the only ones who can be "saved" and partake in the next life, if there is one.

With regard to my own Catholic religion and faith, I have many problems. I would say that due to these problems, my faith has suffered severely and I am at a crisis point—a moment of decision of whether or not to carry on in search of meaning, rationality, and faith in Catholicism. At the moment, largely due to my conservative Catholic upbringing, I have kept up the search for answers to my personal questions concerning Catholicism and Christianity.

Many of my doubts and questions arise concerning Jesus Christ, and these will be discussed later in the paper. I could pursue these questions and doubts of mine for the rest of my life, and I think I will probably wind up doing that. Something tells me, however, that I will eventually find suitable answers to my questions and start to dispel my doubts.

The concept of mystery has played an important part in my life and in my theology. Before I could attempt to search for an answer to the mystery of God, I had to solve the mystery of myself. During my teenage years, the biggest mystery of all for me was the answer to the question, "Who am I?" This was a confusing, uneasy, and yet exciting question to attempt to answer.

The first place I looked was within myself. I would spend many quiet hours reflecting upon my values, attitudes, philosophy, friends, etc., trying to find out who I was. In essence, I wanted to meet myself, for I was a mystery and at the same time the detective trying to solve that mystery.

Gradually, over many years, I was able to reveal myself to myself. I started looking outwards towards other people and discovered a lot about myself through my interactions with others. I became comfortable with myself and the mystery gradually began to disappear. An important point I always kept in mind was that there was an answer to this mystery, and it was only a matter of time before I found it.

Now that I have reasonably solved the mystery of "Who I am," an even more challenging mystery confronts me—that of "Who is God?" or "Is there a God?" Unlike the mystery of who I am, I am not as confident about there being an ultimate understanding of the mystery of God.

In trying to understand and arrive at an understanding of the questions concerning God, I first turned to the teachings of the Catholic church. Up until high school these teachings were enough to satisfy me. During high school, and especially college, I found many weaknesses in the church's teachings. This led me to numerous discussions with many people concerning their beliefs and ideas about God. Those discussions opened my mind and broadened my outlook considerably, but they left me more confused than ever before.

In order to eliminate some of this confusion and get back on the road to solving the mystery, I looked inward to myself. I tried and am still trying to synthesize all the opinions and information I have come across in order to shed some light upon the mystery of God. Quiet personal reflection over a period of time has been my best tool in trying to understand God.

The mystery of God is a challenging and exciting mystery to attempt to solve, but at the same time it is quite frustrating. Unlike the answer to the mystery of myself, I can't be sure that in the end there is an answer to the mystery of God. I can only hope that there is and that I will be able to come to some sort of understanding about it.

Of the two great mysteries in my life, one is virtually solved and the other is seemingly unsolvable. I have come to understand myself, and have started the long road of seeking to understand God.

Although I have not, as of yet, satisfactorily solved the mystery of God for myself, I have come to understand God as the primal and ultimate source of undetermined meaning. There has to be some source of meaning and power greater than that which mankind can give to the world. One need only look to the planets, the galaxies, and even an ordinary human birth to see that surely there is more meaning to life than simply food, shelter and a high-paying job.

Life without meaning is absurd, and it is up to the individual to transcend himself and look for meaning in life. I believe that there is a God and I believe that through God and in God man will find answers to the question of the meaning of life. First man must realize that there is a mystery of meaning, and he must seek an answer to it which will be gradually revealed to him by God. Once this gradual revelation starts to occur, man will gain faith—a personal knowledge of God gained through the experience of God—and will be able to formulate his own theology and beliefs.

Once man accepts God as the One who gives meaning to our lives, he has (as Rahner put it) the fundamental option of saying either "yes" or "no" to God. This choice will determine the orientation of his life as either toward or away from God. This choice is not made in a particular instant; rather it is continually made over time. It is a whole way of life that is manifested by our relationship to God and to fellow human beings.

I have exercised my fundamental option by orienting myself toward and not away from God. As a result of this, I have found some meaning in life and see myself as having an ultimate worth—not just going through the motions—because I have life and am alive by a principle which transcends me: God.

I have always thought of God as a being or spirit who created man and gives him meaning and is around to watch over us. God has always been the ultimate good guy who is the champion of truth, justice and love.

When all else fails, you can always count upon God to support, protect and nourish you.

The "Kingdom of God" is a phrase that I've never felt comfortable with. It seems so pompous, ceremonial and a little bit phoney. Although the actual phrase itself bothers me, some of the concepts behind the phrase do not. If God is to give meaning and direction to our lives, what is to become of this meaning and direction? What is the end result? I think the concept of the Kingdom of God provides a good solution.

As a result of my viewing God as a spirit with the above considerations, a certain type of Kingdom of God comes to mind. My conception of the Kingdom of God is that of a state of being, an idyllic state of being in which we all share in God's love and glory to the fullest extent possible. The final culmination of this kingdom would be our earthly and bodily deaths. At this point, the Kingdom of God would be pretty much what we consider the concept of heaven to be.

I do not view the Kingdom of God as solely an idealistic state to be achieved in the after-life. I believe that the Kingdom is a state of being, and thus is an on-going process that continually strives for culmination in the ideal state. The Kingdom of God is now; it was a month ago, a year ago, two thousand years ago; and it will be tomorrow. I view the Kingdom as starting with the beginning of time and evolving and progressing towards the end of time and its ultimate fulfillment.

An obstacle that impedes the progression of the Kingdom is that of evil. Evil turns man away from God and alienates man from God's love, grace, and meaning. I feel that the key to this problem is time. Eventually the

Kingdom of God will win out; and as time goes on, man seems generally to come closer to the final state of the Kingdom.

Obviously the most central element to Christianity and Catholicism is Jesus himself. I consider myself a Christian and a Catholic, but many of the concepts Christians and Catholics hold cause trouble for me. It is not a case of my disbelieving these concepts; it is a matter of my being skeptical about believing them. It is a fine distinction to make, but only that distinction adequately describes where I am.

Most of my doubts and problems center around Jesus' divinity and resurrection. Specifically, it seems much more plausible and logical to me that Jesus was an ordinary mortal man who preached a good message, but whose friends and followers made him out to be some great hero—made him, in fact, God. An important reason for this viewpoint is that the Gospels, which describe Jesus and all that he did and stood for, were not written until 30-60 years after his death. That appears to be plenty of time to get Jesus' life and death taken all out of context and to read more into them than was there. Even the Bible states that people didn't consider Jesus as God until he had died and left them.

At the present time, I am inclined to believe that Jesus was not God and that he didn't rise from the dead. It is a radical statement for me to make, especially in light of my traditional conservative Catholic upbringing; and I feel slightly uneasy about making it. Whereas most people have problems recognizing the humanity of Christ, my problem is in recognizing his divinity.

I think that Jesus was an ordinary human being just

like any of us, except for the fact that he had a unique
closeness to God. Jesus was the son of God just as you
and I are the sons of God. Jesus was different from
others because he was a radical reformer who changed
people's views concerning religion and the supremacy of
civil law, which often was abusive and put itself in God's
place. Jesus was a unique man in the history of the
world, but I feel that Buddha and the other figures of
Buddhism, Hinduism, and the Moslem worlds also were
unique. What Jesus did for the basically Western culture, others have done for other cultures; and I don't
think that Jesus has supremacy over the others.

To me, it does not matter if Jesus was the absolute or
best revelation of God. To carry it a step farther, it
really doesn't matter to me if Jesus was divine or if he
rose from the dead. It concerns me, of course, but it is
not essential to my following of his teachings. The most
important thing about Christ was his teachings. If the
world should suddenly find out beyond a doubt that
Jesus was not divine and that He did not rise from the
dead, would that radically alter the quality of what he
taught? I would think not.

Jesus' strength lies in his teachings and examples. He
was born in an eye-for-eye time of history and preached
a radical message about love for your fellow man. Jesus
taught others to care for their fellow man and numerous
other good things that were not common practice of the
day. Jesus gave hope and a sense of meaning to countless people. Most importantly, Jesus opened up God to
the people by showing them that God can give people
nourishment, support, and the all-important sense of
meaning in life. Jesus was important in his time, and has

become even more important since his death. One can easily find many testimonies of this.

In time, I may come to accept Jesus' divinity and resurrection. In the meantime I will continue to follow his teachings and examples because they are very worthwhile guidelines upon which to base my life. Even though I have problems with certain concepts of Christianity, I feel that it is the right religious expression for me and that I can be a good Christian; just as one can be a good American without agreeing with the government on everything.

To put everything into perspective, my own theology has been formulated by the many things I have seen, read, heard, and been taught. I have evaluated these experiences and have arrived at my own theology.

To briefly restate some of my basic tenets: I believe there is a God and that God gives meaning to man's existence. I do not really know the meaning of life yet, but I am well on my way to eventually finding a satisfactory answer. While I have trouble accepting Jesus' divinity and resurrection, I believe that Jesus taught mankind some valuable lessons and left us with numerous examples and teachings. I believe that Jesus is worth imitating and following and that is why I am a Christian. I was born into the Catholic faith and see nothing too terribly wrong with it, and that is why I am a Catholic.

I will continue to have doubts throughout my life, and I will continue to seek answers. As these doubts are resolved and answers obtained, my personal theology will become stronger and better.

LIZ KENTRA

AS I sit to write down my personal theology for the first time, it seems to me to be such a complex conglomeration of beliefs, experiences, feelings, questions, and teachings that I do not know where to begin. It is as if someone had asked me to explain how a tapestry was made; but this tapestry is woven with many different threads, by many different artists. Some sections have been rewoven, some discarded. Most confounding of all, though, is the fact that this tapestry has not been completed. In the same way, my theology contains many different beliefs; has been influenced by various individuals, institutions, and experiences; and is not complete. Instead, it is of a dynamic nature which continues to review, unravel and reweave itself.

If I take my first step by viewing my theology as my own interpretation of my personal knowledge of God which has been gained through my experience of God, things begin to simplify. For I have experienced God. In class, we spoke of depth experiences as situations or events which have special meaning or significance for us as individuals. I have experienced these situations under joyful conditions with delight and awe, and under mournful conditions with anger and awe. Regardless of the conditions, however, these experiences have been my encounters with the mystery that is God. Whether I have been amazed while studying the intricacies of life and human emotion, distraught at the pain and suffering of others I have seen or heard about, or filled with joy at a particularly beautiful liturgy, I have gotten glimpses of a powerful, larger mystery, a guiding force, an ultimate meaning. This mystery called God does not offer meaning for just myself, however, but for mankind and this world in general.

It's not that I understand this world or humankind —or myself for that matter—because I believe in God. To be honest, I have no idea why he made the human condition the way it is. (It seems to me it would have been a lot easier to have stopped with angels.) Despite my lack of understanding, however, I believe in the meaning of my life, of mankind, and of the world in general as being created by God and existing with some sort of function and worth. I also believe that I have a mission or goal in life, and that is to strive for a better understanding of and a closeness with the Creator who is the meaning of my life.

In believing in God, in identifying my meaning with him, and in accepting the challenge to orient my life towards him, I am conscious of my personal response to what Rahner calls the fundamental option. My personal idea of the fundamental option differs from Rahner's, however. Where Rahner believes it to be the radical orientation of one's whole life toward or away from God, I think it is more of a belief in God and an acceptance of the challenge to orient your whole life toward him. I do not think you can say a person who commits sin has his or her life completely oriented to God. Rather, an individual makes that initial orientation towards God by deciding his or her beliefs, morals, and values, and then strives to complete that commitment by extending that orientation throughout the spiritual self *and* the actions of that individual.

Along with this challenge to total commitment, God

has given man several means to help in his understanding of God and to facilitate his struggle on earth. Affecting us most directly in our everyday lives are the ability to transcend, the continuous gift of grace, and Jesus Christ.

As humans, we are able to think, reason, philosophize, love, and hate. We are thus able to transcend the tangible while still maintaining immanence to ourselves and to the world around us. Failure to recognize, exercise, and develop our ability to transcend and, at the same time, to maintain immanence is a denial of one of the fundamental abilities that distinguish us as human. A failure of a human to develop either transcendence or immanence results in an underdeveloped personality; either the person is in the clouds all the time with no grasp of reality, or he or she is incapable of looking beyond himself or herself and the concreteness of things to enter into relationships and realize the abstract entities in human life. Thus God reveals himself through the gift of transcendence in a primary way in our search for meaning and in a continuous way in the mystery we encounter through transcendence.

As God reveals himself and his mystery to us through our ability to transcend, he reveals himself to us in another way through grace and revelation. I believe grace, or God's self-communication to us, is a present and on-going process; and the realization of this is one of the most necessary tenets for believers in the world today. Our world is not static; our lives are not static. In order to be relevant and helpful, therefore, God's messages are not static. Both grace and revelation are continuous opportunities that God makes available to us to increase our knowledge of him and of ourselves. Our responses to these opportunities reflect the commitment or lack of commitment we have made to the challenge of God's fundamental option.

Revelation is available to us in a multitude of forms, ranging from prayer to interactions with others to the Bible and church dogma. I believe revelation can be direct or mediated by the visible things in our lives. Revelation in an unmediated form is no less mysterious than mediated revelation; it is God's mysterious self-communication to individuals through direct channels such as private prayer and conscience. Revelation in a mediated form is often difficult to recognize. Aside from the more obvious sources and products of revelation such as history and dogma, there are numerous interactions we are involved in daily through which we can encounter grace without recognizing it or being aware of our response.

If we hold that our identity and the meaning of our lives are found in God, then anything affecting who we are takes on a religious dimension. The challenge of God is an all-encompassing one which extends into all facets of our lives. Therefore we cannot separate elements of our world and our lives into two types: those having religious dimensions and those not having religious dimensions. Instead, we must recognize that all we see and are connected with has something to do with our relationship to God and, therefore, has a potential role in revelation.

God's revelation has established its full potentiality in Jesus Christ. The unrestricted nature of man makes it possible for him to open up to this revelation potentiality of the infinity of God without changing his nature.

The hypostatic union is the ultimate form of grace, creating teachings, inspiration, and a supreme role model for men in Jesus Christ. As a man, Jesus utilized the pathways God has given men, transcendence and grace, and fully developed the potentiality of God's self-communication until he became one with that self-communication. Having accepted the challenge of the fundamental option, I think Jesus alone succeeded in orienting his *whole* life toward God.

This complete orientation was the perfection of all the God-oriented humanity of Christ (for I think there are detrimental aspects of humanity, such as jealousy and doubt, in addition to the God-oriented aspects of humanity), which enabled him to reach divinity, complete identification with God. Through studying and seeking an understanding of Jesus, we are seeking God's self-communication.

I don't know if Jesus knew of his divinity or if he understood the mystery of God. I am not convinced of the importance of those questions. Christology, whether from below or from above, is an attempt to explain the incarnation, which is itself a mystery. My own view of Jesus Christ is a merger of the two Christologies. I think that Jesus knew he was divine before the resurrection, but that knowledge did not alter his humanity. I also think he knew of his destiny here on earth, but that knowledge did not alter his humanity either. The important fact to me is that we can find the self-communication of God in the tangible life of Jesus Christ.

Jesus emphasized in his teachings the Kingdom of God. Before our coverage of the Kingdom of God in class, I regarded it only as the reign of God. I now understand the Kingdom of God to be not only the reign of God, but also the presence of God in us and in the world as a reconciling spirit bringing all things to him, and as the movement toward fulfillment of this reconciliation, the reign of God.

This view of the Kingdom of God as a process which is present today is a source of hope and encouragement to the believers on earth. I find it difficult to recognize the world's movement toward the Kingdom of God, however. It seems to me that the world has been regressing in its morals and actions in the past century, rather than moving toward an omega point of final reconciliation with God. Perhaps my view is limited or distorted by a lack of distance from the subject or by a lack of a panoramic view of the world. I do believe this omega point of reconciliation is a reality of the future, even if I cannot see the movement toward it in my world.

I believe the Catholic Church is a part of the Kingdom of God as an on-going source of reconciliation between God and man. As God has given man transcendence, grace, and the Savior, God also has given man a continuous means to know and serve him better in the Catholic Church. I do not think other religions are invalid in this respect, but the Catholic Church alone has been established on earth by Jesus Christ and thus offers revelation and is able to demythologize that revelation in a unique way. I think we have an obligation to remain followers of this church and work to realize any changes we think necessary in it. The church *is* the community of followers and, as mature Catholics, we have the responsibility to think independently. Differences or conflicts with the church should be shared or evaluated for the perfection of our individual faith and of the church.

They are not reasons to abandon the church and find another one more compatible with the beliefs in conflict.

As a community, the church is dynamic, changing. It should reflect and meet the needs and concerns of its members. That will not happen, however, unless its members work within the church and with the hierarchy to express those needs and concerns. This is our responsibility as mature Catholics: to continually evaluate our needs and the church and to work for the most effective church with the help of the Holy Spirit.

Unfortunately, with all of the rituals and dogma of the church, many Catholics lose sight of this responsibility and of the goal of the Church—complete reconciliation of God and man. Somehow God and Jesus Christ are lost or removed from our consciousness. Our concern is with following the rules and completing the formula instead of with establishing a basic and lasting relationship with God. Since the Catholic Church's rituals and rules were established for the purpose of providing a way to know, worship, and serve God, blind following of the rules of the church defeats the purpose of those rules. To have faith, or to have a personal knowledge of and relationship with God, you must take responsibility for your beliefs. This means continuous re-evaluation and challenge of those beliefs. In this way, I do not think a personal theology can ever be complete if an individual questions and re-evaluates his or her faith. Instead, that person's relationship with God is changing, hopefully growing, into a new tapestry of faith.

ROBERT KEMPF

THEOLOGICAL ANTHROPOLOGY is a way of studying God by studying man. Specifically, by reflecting upon myself and my perceptions, I have gained a greater understanding of God and his works. This personal theological review begins with a discussion of **mystery,** then a look at **preconceptions,** followed by a section on **transcendence** and some speculative thoughts on **evil.** It concludes with some of my thoughts about Jesus Christ from the point of view of ascending **Christology.**

Mystery is inevitable in human existence. We can not know exactly who we are or why we are here. I ask myself: What is it all about? What should I do? Why do I feel as I do? These questions seem to lead to more questions and so on. The mystery in life seems never-ending.

What, then, is reality? I experience the world through my five senses. I can see, feel, hear, taste and smell the world; but do I sense the same world as anyone else? For example, suppose I see a color and recognize it to be green. I make this association between the hue I perceive, the one I have been taught to call green, and the actual word "green." Could it be possible that someone else perceives an entirely different hue, which I might call "blue," coming from the same source as the "green" I see? It could be that different people see specific world characteristics in completely different ways; but all can communicate because of their learned association between the stimuli, different as they may be, and the communicative devices. Although scientific evidence may contradict this example, it gives a good analogical picture of the problem of the concept of reality.

The problem with reality is that there is more than one. The word "reality" implies a uniquely true fact or essence of an object or concept. But one man's reality is another man's myth. People perceive the same world in a multitude of different ways. And so *reality is a mystery*. I can never completely or positively check my reality against the reality of another human being. I must be my own judge of what exists, why it is there, who put it there, and ultimately, who I am.

Who I am seems to be the most basic question I can ask. Socrates said, "Know thyself;" but can anyone really know who he or she is? To know oneself is to know where one comes from. This is a mystery. I do not know exactly where I or the universe as a whole originated. People have always searched for the answer to where they came from. Some resolve this mystery with another mystery by claiming God as the source of their being. Others choose to avoid the question and still others focus on the short term question, "Where did I come from one hundred thousand years ago?"

The only full answer to the mystery of who I am is found in another mystery: God. This is because the basic question of who I am is really a question of the meaning of life. Meaning comes from the creator and God is our creator. I experience God through my creation and my interaction with his creation. How then can I better experience God and by what method do I come to know him?

Just as mystery can seem to be at the core of everything that we know, **preconceptions** can filter all which we experience. In class, we spoke of preconceptions. We discussed how the preconceptions of Catholics, meaning their frames of reference, have changed over the life span of the church. Medieval church doctrine viewed human existence objectively, as unchanging and unaffected by history. Modern theologians focus on the consciousness of the human person as a cocreator with God. This shift in Catholic thought (that is, the change in the preconceptions of Catholics as individuals rather than the strict teaching of the Church) is something that I have thought much about. We have gone from viewing God as supernatural, far above and away from people, to God revealing himself through the grace present in people. I have held both views with conviction, each at different points in my life.

I know God better than I know anyone else, and he knows me better than I know myself. I see him in the eyes of a person with drive, committed to his or her goals and headstrong with pride. I see him in a baby's first curl of hair, in a wind that whispers in my ear, in the look in my mother's eyes. God has given me everything. It is all good. I often think some things are bad, later to find their hidden good. I still do not know why he lets soldiers kill babies. I know God better than I know any single person or thing, but I still do not understand him.

And God knows me. He knows when I am doing what will later make me unhappy. He showed me how terrible sadness and anger are in the world just after I hurt my brother's feelings. He reassures me when I make the right move. Just as I finished teaching one of the new freshmen in the trumpet section how to march the hike step, he opened my mind to recall my freshman year and the joy I felt from being in the marching band. God knows me better than anyone else.

God seems to be the goodness revealed through other people, myself, and the concrete world; and God also seems to be far away, distant, detached and above. Sure God is here, in my life and in the world; but I can't truly describe who he is. I have never touched him or heard him speak aloud. I am also not so sure that people always deserve the goodness God provides. It seems as though God is not around to mind the shop. I use my freedom to hurt others and groups of people use their freedom to take away the freedom of others. God seems far away.

I guess it is my own preconception, my world view, that determines where God is for me. That preconception came from my environment, something I was not initially free to choose. But my world view changes, just as the preconceptions of Catholics as a group have changed. Maybe preconceptions are what limit us, as it is change in these preconceptions that really makes us search for God, whether he be far above or in our midst.

Preconceptions then, can block our ability to reach outside ourselves. They restrict our nature for **transcendence.** "Transcend" comes from the Latin words "trans" meaning over and "scandere" meaning to climb. So in writing about transcendence I am dealing with a climbing over, a going outside myself across physical boundaries, a reaching beyond the world of material objects for the limitless. Karl Rahner refers to transcendence as an element within all our experience in the world, one which is intrinsic to our "two-directional" knowledge and human freedom.

Rahner states that all of our experience of the world is also simultaneously an experience of the self. He says that we have a "two-directional" knowledge, and by this he means that our act of knowing is a conscious process. So in effect, to know an object is to know ourselves knowing the object. By this we transcend to spiritual existence.

For me, this "two-directional" knowledge is not something I often think of. Right now I am thinking that it is 7:07 AM, I have a class at 8 AM, and I am not done with this section of my paper yet. As I reflect upon what I have just written, I see that my mind is wandering. So in this sense of knowing my feelings and thoughts about the world, which right now are to finish this section of my paper and make it to class on time, I am transcending the situation. This makes me feel good. I am not a computer programmed to churn out Theology papers. I am more. I think that it is this feeling of more that puts me in touch with God.

Rahner cites human freedom as another clue to our transcendence. He acknowledges that we are determined genetically, environmentally and so on, but he asserts that we are free to choose who we shall be, free to choose an identity. To the extent that we are free and possess "two-directional" knowledge of the world, we exist outside the finite world. This metaphysical existence is transcendence.

My experience with freedom, my personal human freedom, is very clear to me. I was raised in a family which placed emphasis on getting an education, hard work, and doing one's best. But I was the one who got up at 6:00 AM this morning to type this paper. No one coerced me into this. No one gave me a wake up call. I set the alarm myself. In fact, the more I show myself that I am free, for example by making choices that are not easy, the more control I feel over my life and the more I transcend it.

So, what I have done is to reflect upon my own ideas and those of Karl Rahner. In doing this I have transcended my physical presence at my desk at this point in time. Transcendence is what I am experiencing now by freely choosing to look back on what I have written and knowing that I am doing so. In reflection, I find transcendence.

I have thus far dealt with mystery, preconceptions, and transcendence. My next topic is not so cut and dried. For, as the reader will see, **evil** is something we can only speculate about. Many things happen in this world that just do not make sense. Young people die of cancer, children are kidnapped and killed by lunatics, and innocent people are slaughtered in war. It seems to me that if God is God—that is, if God is all-powerful and all-knowing—he would not let evil prevail in the world. Taking this one step further, if God is the creator of all, then why would God create evil? For if God is truly the creator, truly omnipotent and truly omniscient, he must have consciously created evil. If he did not create evil, he is not God. Then why is it that God should will evil upon the world?

My only answer to this question is that by creating this thing we call evil, God, being all good, spared us from something worse: a lack of freedom. This lack of freedom would mean a sort of slavery of the mind. I think if we did not have evil, if we did not have a distinction between good and bad, we could not be free as individuals. Our destiny would have been determined by God.

God did not create us as robots. He created us in his image, that is, he created us freely and in turn made us autonomous and free like himself. No one is completely determined. No occurrence is completely predictable. Life is dynamic, changing with each new discovery, transition, and decision. People become whatever they make themselves to be through their fundamental option.

This fundamental option is basically the way each individual chooses to live his or her life. This personal choice of life style is an experience available to all. What matters is that we have a choice. This means that there can always be hope for good over evil.

What then could the terrible tragedies of losing a son to cancer or seeing a sister killed by a drunk driver mean? These incidents seem to take away our freedom. It seems that there is nothing we can do to stop them. I think that these awful things hold a message for us from God. God might be saying something like this: "I created you, I love you, and you are free; but never forget why you are on earth. You must love others as I have loved you, today, because you may not have the chance tomorrow." Maybe this is why we have evil in the world.

All the previous subjects seem to lead to **Christology**. Although it seems to be the most important, I find the study of Jesus Christ to be the farthest from me. We

study Christ as historical and biblical. We have historical accounts by Josephus the historian, Pliny the
younger, and Tacitus. We have biblical accounts by the
evangelists Mark, Matthew, Luke and John. The church
teaches that Jesus was both totally God and totally man.
We have many sources and teachings to tell us who
Jesus should be to us, but who he is to me and what does
he mean in my life?

Jesus is a statue. He comes wrapped in a golden pack-
age, with tissue paper surrounding his plaster of Paris
body. He sits on my mother's dresser, and she keeps a
five or a ten dollar bill under him so she can never spend
all her money in one place. My rosary, the one that be-
longed to my Grampa, has a figure of Christ on the
cross. I see Jesus on his cross more than in any other
setting. I guess people are trying to tell the world that it
is OK to suffer, maybe that it is even good to suffer.

I wonder what Jesus has to say about all these images
of himself. Perhaps he would be angry that most of the
images portray sadness and suffering. Maybe this is
what he wants. Maybe he doesn't know.

I know the Jesus of the Bible. He preached the Kingdom of God. He healed the sick, comforted the lonely,
raised the dead, and generally tried to give people a
peaceful feeling. He said that the Kingdom of God is
upon us and because of this we are already saved if we
trust in God, or at least this is what I've been taught.

I think Jesus is God, and other times I think he is
man; but I find it very difficult to see Jesus as both
totally human and totally divine at the same time. I'm
not sure what to think. He seems to be both, but how
could he be totally God and totally man at the same

time? Rahner's explanation is that Jesus was God because of his total acceptance of humanity. I understand Rahner's explanation, but I am still unsettled about it.

All in all, Jesus is a symbol for me. What I know of his life serves as an example to me for how I should live my life. Living like Jesus seems to make me feel closer to God.

This personal theological review began with a discussion of **mystery,** then covered **preconceptions,** followed by a section on **transcendence.** Some speculative thoughts were given on **evil,** and I concluded with some of my thoughts on Jesus Christ from the point of view of ascending **Christology.** By reflecting upon myself and my perceptions, I have gained a greater understanding of God and his works.

BRIAN SHANNON

WHEN I found out at the beginning of the semester that our final paper would entail stating my personal theology, I must admit that I was less than enthusiastic. At that time, I could not even imagine what I would write about. There were so many things pertaining to my faith of which I was ignorant, and many things which I could not bring myself to accept. Our class has been greatly informative and has even helped me to accept certain facets of the Catholic faith.

I am a skeptic at heart; I must be quite sure of something before I will adhere to it. So there are many aspects of my faith which I am not yet ready to embrace. That is not to say that I totally reject certain ideas, it is just that I may not yet be convinced of the true motivation for believing such ideas. With this in mind, I will attempt to examine and express my personal feelings on several important ideas concerning the Catholic faith.

A logical place to start is with *the* central person of Christian life, Jesus Christ himself. The subject of Jesus is one which is key to the lives of Catholics, but is also a subject which is often accepted without reason or unconditionally by these same Catholics.

The most common view of Jesus held by Catholics is that of the Son of God. Contained in this view are the ideas of the Immaculate Conception, Mary as the Mother of God, Joseph as Jesus' father on earth, and so on. The incidents surrounding the birth of this man called Jesus neatly followed the plan laid forth in the writings and teachings of prophets who taught prior to Christ's birth. Although some of these incidents were not meant to be taken literally and thus are chiefly symbolic, the idea of the Lord God sending his human form to earth to offer the Kingdom of God is remarkable, almost incomprehensible.

I have often considered the view held by many people that this man called Jesus Christ could not have been the Son of God, that he in fact was a prophet. Many have claimed that he was the greatest of prophets, with an apparent power to perform miracles. I believed in this idea of Jesus as prophet for quite a while.

Two years ago, when I began making my own decisions concerning my faith, I came to realize the importance and the centrality of Jesus. Although there are certain things with respect to Jesus that I am not ready to accept, the process of demythologization has allowed me to understand the meaning behind some symbolic events regarding Jesus which I took as meaningless not too long ago.

Now, after being exposed to many differing views of the Catholic Church, I realize that Jesus indeed is the central factor to my faith. Bearing this in mind, I see that Jesus had to be much more than just a prophet. For me, Jesus had to be the Son of God. No mere prophet could have accomplished as much or have had such an impact on mankind as Jesus did. What set this man apart from other men was his divinity, the fact that he was the Lord God's representation in human form.

In deciding who Jesus was for me, I found it amazing that such a delicate balance between humanity and divinity could be struck. Jesus was human enough to be accepted by and to be able to relate to all levels of men, from kings to beggars. Also, he had a sense of divinity, manifested through his miracles and teachings, which led people to realize that he was special—if not the son of God, then certainly a fulfilling prophet.

So I can accept the idea that this man Jesus was the Son of God. I can also accept the idea of the human/ divine dual nature of Jesus. What I still have a problem dealing with is the Kingdom of God which Jesus sought to guide mankind toward. No one can know with any certainty what this kingdom is like, but after hearing many different ideas, I have seen too many inconsistencies to be able to formulate any solid beliefs of my own about the Kingdom of God.

In class we were presented with the notion that the concept of the Kingdom of God is based on the premise that human nature alone cannot sustain itself in justice, peace, and harmony. We also were exposed to the idea that the Kingdom of God is in a process of evolution toward perfection. The implication of this was that since the Kingdom of God is evolving, then this Kingdom is present here and now on earth. If this is the case, then I wish someone would spread the word to the people of Lebanon, El Salvador, and Northern Ireland.

After giving the aforementioned ideas concerning the Kingdom of God considerable thought, I realize that I just cannot accept them. We defined the Kingdom of God as a condition or state where God's name is blessed, his will is done, and the poor and downtrodden are cared for. Although this definition is not the only one and may be meant to be idealistic, it probably adequately captures the essence of the Kingdom of God. If this is the case, then I cannot say that the world I live in resembles a condition or state such as this, and my world is relatively good. Certainly in some circles God's name *is* blessed and his will *is* done, but there are so many contrary conditions present today that I cannot believe that the Kingdom of God exists here and now in any form.

To me, the Kingdom of God is something to which we as followers of Christ must aspire. Juvenile as it may sound, I believe the Kingdom must be earned. Once a Christian realizes this, then the idea of the Kingdom becomes the ultimate motivation and the ultimate rationale for many actions and decisions regarding faith. People view the Kingdom of God as the reason why they are kind to others and why they go to mass each week; they hope to enjoy eternal life in God's Kingdom. There is nothing wrong with this way of thinking, but it should not be the sole reason for why we care for others. I see God's Kingdom as the meaning for which I have searched and will continue to search.

When I say the Kingdom is a source of meaning for me, I do not intend to imply that I find meaning in everything. My understanding of the church's view is that whether consciously or not, meaning should be present in all of our actions, and if we look for this meaning hard enough, we find God. Well, I personally believe that many people get carried away trying to find meaning in everything when sometimes there may be none. I can certainly see a *purpose* in almost everything, but I do not see the words "purpose" and "meaning" as synonymous. Whether a person is Catholic or not, the idea of meaning should be related to some higher power. Since I believe meaning is related to a higher power, then anyone who does not have faith in a god, any god, cannot find or will not try to find meaning in anything.

But ultimately the quest for meaning, which is the most important quest, must be personal. It is a special search; answers cannot be given by family, friends, or even the clergy. To look for meaning is to wrestle with a question which has been answered for many, but which also may hold no answer for me: Why am I here?

If the above thoughts on meaning are somewhat cloudy, the reason is that I am not quite sure about the ultimate meaning of my life. I was always told as a child to do this or that for God; and if I was not doing it for God, then my meaning became my parents and my family. However, realizing the finiteness of our earthly lives, the meaning for me has reverted back to God. There must be more to meaning than the selfish reason of attaining eternal life in God's Kingdom.

I often chalk up my failure to realize an ultimate meaning to the mystery of God. Volumes have been written attempting to find an answer to the question of who God is. About one year ago, when I was in the throes of my radical stage concerning faith, I concluded that God was no more than a convenient state of mind. I felt God was simply a diversion from our lives and a very good way to explain so many things both good and bad. For a time, I used to think that people must be crazy to believe in something so intangible and unexplainable. Clearly, I thought I had all the answers.

Eventually I realized how very wrong I was. That is not to say I have unraveled the mystery of God; as far as I know, no one has. But I now see, largely through observation of others and searching myself, that God must be more than simply a state of mind. For me, God is a mysterious type of order in an otherwise chaotic life.

Right or wrong, my God is a crutch; but He is not an ex-
cuse. (It is just as absurd to say "God made me do it" as
it is to say "The devil made me do it.")

Many of my personal ideas concerning my faith have
undergone substantial change in the two years that I
have been away from "the nest." One of these ideas
concerns revelation. I used to be convinced that a revelation was a very dramatic occurrence which affected
some favored person. The story of St. Paul's being
knocked down by a lightning bolt used to exemplify my
former notion of revelation.

Now, through what I have learned from class and
through my ability to make my own decisions, I have
come to see revelation as a type of dialogue which is
created when any person is open to God's communication, whether this communication occurs in another's
smile or in a picturesque sunset. Since this is a dialogue,
however, a response must be generated. If God chooses
to reveal himself and his power through such mediators,
then it should only be natural to make a response.

The way in which I respond to God's revelation is perhaps only the first step in the lifelong process of accounting for my existence. I first must be open to God
as he makes himself known to me in countless ways:
through nature, through people, etc. I can honestly say I
have been open to these mediators. My type of openness
has often harmed me in dealing with people; but with
God, my openness has been a real plus.

I presently find myself at the stage in which a great
many people my age find themselves. I now must
choose, after considering many things, whether I can

find joy and meaning in God and Jesus Christ. I must wrestle with this, for a decision of this magnitude which comes too easily could be suspect. Often I ask myself why such a choice is so vital, and I quickly receive an answer when I observe people (not only clergy) whose sole motivator is God.

Once I finally decide whether God is my meaning or not—there is no middle ground—the decision is both a beginning and an end. It marks the end of the period in which I have struggled with the most basic question of faith. And it also represents the beginning of the process of finding out who God really is to me. Thus, a type of freedom is involved.

Just as this freedom to choose and to decide emerges, so do certain restraints connected with growing up in contemporary Catholic America. Pressure caused chiefly by the economy has caused a massive swing from great emphasis on religion to greater emphasis on the individual. This increased individualism has been forced on us, in the sense that we have merely reacted to pressures which have made survival, let alone advancement, an important goal. The increased concern for things of a temporal nature has tended to force religion into "the back seat."

To sum up so far, I believe that my faith centers around Jesus Christ and the message he brought. He was the Son of God and he told of the Kingdom of God which I do not believe is present on this earth. Also, I am searching for the elusive meaning to my life.

Well, those are interesting topics of conversation and they look good on paper, but what do they mean with regard to my actions and attitudes toward others? In other words, what are my responsibilities to both my God and my fellow man?

In general, all of us are simply responsible for treating and loving others as we ourselves would wish to be treated and loved. That is quite a simple statement, and one which is not followed by people in the way it was meant to be followed. (If some of this sounds a bit self-righteous, I would like to say that I am guilty of all the implied sins contained within these pages.)

I see my personal responsibility as greater than this. I have been fortunate enough to have been given many things, the greatest of which I consider to be my abilities to deal with people. Since I have been given these things, I should give that much more to God. The best way of showing my devotion to God is to love and care for others. Up to this point, I feel I have not lived up to my potential for serving God and others. Selfish reasons have often led me to ignore others while at the same time only going through the motions when it came to God.

Religion for me has entailed a series of increased responsibilities. Once I had virtually no responsibility other than to follow the orders of my parents or teachers. Now that I am semi-detached from my parents and free to make many religious decisions, I am more responsible for my religious well-being and for the contribution to God which I am supposed to make. And as I grow older and more free to act on my own volition, I will be responsible for giving even more to my faith and to others, possibly even to a wife and children.

As this responsibility and my potential contribution increase, the magnitude of my fundamental decision to either accept God or reject God becomes clearer. Simply put, my choice to accept God must be the most important decision I have made or ever will make. Although I am not always conscious of it, God is the primary driving force in my life. He should be my meaning, but I would not have been able to see this if it were not for the example of his son, Jesus Christ.

So I have many questions and reservations about my faith, and I like to think that there are others in the same boat. What is vital, though, is that I accept and embrace God and his son Jesus. I have never been a great one for listening to religious oratory, but I am sincere when I say that being able to accept Jesus Christ has given me strength. With this strength, I feel confident that I will find answers to the many questions I have. For the first time in my life, I am enjoying responsibility and looking forward to challenging it. I can attribute this to Jesus. And my reasons for helping others and showing devotion to God are not selfish.

In sum, I am finally comfortable and happy with my faith. I cannot say that my faith is perfect; but, like the Kingdom of God, my faith is in the process of evolution toward perfection.

GREGORY BOHDAN

THEOLOGY. The word brings to mind such concepts as church, Jesus Christ, and God for most Christians, and to many church members this word means a rigid set of religious do's and don't's. The more progressive concept of theology, however, is not defined as a written set of rules, but rather as the interpretation of one's faith. This newer concept allows theology to be more highly personalized, and makes it necessary that each individual work at formulating and interpreting his own form of theology. This contemporary form of theology is in direct contrast to the more traditional "black box" form which the church preached and attempted to impose on its members. This paper is an attempt to outline and defend my personal theology, which is based on my theological background and on newly acquired religious concepts.

Of course, one's religious upbringing has a tremendous influence on the shaping of a personal theology, so that a brief explanation of my religious background is necessary to establish a basis, or a reference point, on which my theology may be understood. I was baptized in the Lutheran Church and brought up in contact with its beliefs and religious interpretations. Through religion classes I was able to acquire an adequate understanding of basic religious concepts such as God, Jesus Christ, and the Kingdom of God; however, this understanding was typically drawn from some textbook definition, and was rarely ever explained from the ground up. Since the Lutheran Church was my only contact with religion, my theology grew from common church understandings and therefore closely resembled the theologies of most other Lutherans.

This soon changed after I began four years at a Catholic-run and predominantly Catholic-attended university. Religious beliefs differing from my own are quite common here at Notre Dame, and have prompted me to reevaluate and sometimes alter my own beliefs. Overall, being subjected to two separate religious faiths has taught me to be open-minded and to expand my theology in terms of both the Lutheran and the Catholic churches. With this in mind, then, it is not surprising that I am very receptive to most well-explained religious concepts.

One goal common to all religions is the attempt to provide an explanation of the meaning of existence, since by definition all human beings have meaning. The meaning of human existence is, for the most part, shrouded in mystery; but through careful step-by-step study the answer to the basic question "Who am I?" may be revealed. Only after this question is answered may a theology be further explored in terms of the church, Jesus Christ, and God. A detailed study of these three terms and other closely related terms shows how these concepts are intricately related and how they progressively provide a foundation on which to base a theology.

A concept very basic to my theology is that of secularization, which is defined as a process of moving away from a religious answer to every human problem and toward the acceptance of substantial responsibility for the quality of human life. Thus, secularization is literally a general change in the belief of a person or group of people, or a common movement from that of pre-destiny to that of self-destiny. Secularization ultimately leads to a decline in the power of the church, with this power being transferred instead to social sciences like psychology, sociology, and anthropology.

Still, neither the social sciences nor religion can explain all human problems. The social sciences often yield clues to the origins of many human problems, un-ravelling bits of "unknown mystery." Hence, this secularization eliminates many non-mysteries from our lives and leads to better definition and strengthening of true mysteries, all the while intensifying the belief that some mysteries may be explained by religion only. Sec-ularization, therefore, does not undermine religion, as might be initially thought, but actually serves to clarify its purpose. Without secularization, religion would be incorrectly employed to explain all the problems of society, and the scope of religion would be too wide to properly explain the true mysteries of life.

Once the usefulness and limitations of religion are understood, the question "Who am I?" may be dis-cussed. The philosopher Descartes with his famous phrase "Cogito Ergo Sum" gave the world a proof for the **existence** of self, but failed to apply the same genius in discovering the **meaning** of self. Descartes arrived at his proof for existence on a purely logical plane of cog-nizance, but an extensive search reveals that the answer to the question of the meaning of existence is not found on this plane.

The assumption that the meaning of existence of self is unthematic and somehow related to God provides a much-needed basis for understanding. God is an immanent force in our lives and somehow must be the explanation of the meaning of the existence of self. More specifically, God is the meaning of who Greg Bohdan is. This belief requires knowledge of the concept of transcendence, but above all requires faith. Faith is defined as the personal knowledge of God gained through the experience of God (i.e., a personal relationship). In conclusion, to reach ultimate understanding of our situation, we must have faith.

Before the relevance and meaning of faith are discussed, it is helpful to understand how faith is sometimes focused through the church. The church as an institution provides for close theological study of religion and provides a medium through which the public is taught this religion. The church plays an important role in discovering the meaning of the existence of self by facilitating the study of various concepts necessary to formulate a personal theology. However, before the church and its related beliefs may be accepted, the foundations on which the church (meaning the Christian Church) is built must be accepted. These foundations, which are at the core of the church, are Jesus Christ and God, both of which are discussed later in this paper. Yet the explanation of the church as a means of focusing faith is straightforward and easily understood.

Faith, as a means by which to know God, is a concept that holds a unique personal meaning for every individual. Faith may be thought of as the acceptance of God and one's belief in what God wills. Historically, faith in the Christian Church has taken on several distinct forms as a result of the influence of varying sociological conditions. Thus, faith is necessarily a dynamic concept, since it must answer religious questions and justify actions of people in their real-life world. As the world about them changes, people must re-evaluate what they are looking for in terms of specifics of faith. For instance, if a particular culture dictates that great public concern should be shown towards death and dying, then that community must maintain a form of faith that in some manner attempts to explain or rationalize this unpleasant subject in terms of one's personal relationship with God. In this manner the form of faith is ever-changing, keeping pace with the evolving forms of culture.

What if faith were an unchanging and rigid set of beliefs? As time passed and culture evolved, faith in this rigid form would become meaningless or at best hollow, since many of the cultural ideals on which it was based would be missing and already replaced by more modern and pertinent ideals. Some forms of faith are held captive in the "black box," until they are removed, modified, and later replaced. Some religious groups traditionally maintain the "old form" of faith until they recognize a cultural change as a valid and progressive change, deserving consideration in the next reformulation of the contemporary concept of faith. Then "the box" is opened, and the concept is adjusted and promptly returned to the box. This method, while drawing some criticism from the more progressive sector of society, is an effective and necessary method of organizing a consistent, world-wide church. As a result, this step-like reformulation of faith is both a necessary and a viable process.

Faith usually changes in a positive direction; that is, faith in God is usually strengthened. Generally, as time passes, faith is reinforced through one's religious education as well as through one's real-life experiences, particularly through depth experiences. Depth experiences are those which are memorable, provide a source of decision, and tend to unify one's life. An outstanding example of a depth experience is the death of a close friend or relative. This tragic event forces one to re-evaluate his priorities and provokes a renewed search for meaning in life. Above all, faith in God and in all he represents is strengthened—maybe as a result of hoping that he will care for the deceased, but probably as a result of the renewed search for ultimate meaning and guidance in one's life. It is this strong belief in his righteousness and ability to guide us that instills faith.

Another concept that helps to intensify the understanding of God, as well as strengthen our faith, is that of grace. Theologians have differing definitions and concepts of grace, but Karl Rahner best explains the process and simplifies the understanding. He defines grace as God's self-communication to us, his people, and as the effects of that self-communication. This self-communication is delivered through revelation. Grace, he explains, can be broken down into two categories: uncreated and created grace. Uncreated grace is God himself dwelling within us all, while created grace is something above human power and understanding which is given freely to us all.

The important aspect of both types of grace is that grace is said to be *given* to all, although not necessarily *received*. It is my understanding that uncreated grace, or God's existence within us, is at all times with each and every one of us so that we are always in his grace. However, created grace is a gift earned through our beliefs and actions and serves to strengthen our freedom (meaning self-realization) and knowledge (meaning the understanding and the love of God). Thus, as we receive this offer of created grace, we grow spiritually in terms of both freedom and knowledge, which in turn brings us closer to the ultimate understanding of the meaning of our existence. Created grace therefore dictates that some individuals receive more grace than others, but deservedly so. God initiates the relationship with us through his grace, and we respond with our developing faith.

As I stated before, Jesus Christ along with God is the foundation of the Christian Church and must be understood before the church may be accepted in its present form. The study of Jesus Christ, or Christology, consists of two different approaches: ascending and descending. The more traditional or fundamentalist approach, descending Christology, begins with Jesus Christ as the son of God and a member of the trinity, and only later reveals how Jesus was also a historical human being. The more progressive approach, ascending Christology, begins with Jesus as a man in history and gradually reveals him as the son of God. Ascending Christology requires another concept, that of matter and spirit; and it allows for the introduction of the key concept of the Kingdom of God. Spirit in this context should not be confused with the older, more specific term "soul," which may be applied only to human beings. Spirit instead refers to all forces, including the soul, that hold matter in specific forms and allow these objects to maintain their existence. Ascending Christology holds that matter and spirit evolve simultaneously and move towards a common goal, possibly the Kingdom of God, and only there can true meaning for existence of self found.

Understanding Jesus' life itself, as well as the method by which it is studied, is useful in shaping a personal theology. Jesus the son of God and Jesus the influential man both refer to the same being, but they differ as a result of the perspective taken. Both perspectives are valid, but the resulting explanations of Jesus as divine and Jesus as human seem to raise some serious discrepancies. Thus if both viewpoints are to be held as valid and useful, an attempt must be made to explain one perspective in the light of the other in some logical, continuous manner. The problem arises because the word "divine" implies infinity, and man does not have a capacity for the infinite. Or does he? If man does have this capacity, then perhaps Jesus, since he was without original sin, may have attained this perfection in the form of divinity.

Careful study reveals that the results of this reasoning are sometimes confusing and often vague; yet the reasoning is partially satisfactory in attempting to explain the question of Jesus' human and divine characteristics. Further thought on this question leads to the realization that it is not a contradiction in answers that is the problem, but rather that the question itself is improper. Christianity is not concerned so much with the origin of Jesus Christ, as with his meaning for existence.

In this light, the concepts of Jesus as divine and Jesus as human may be easily explained and may even complement one another. For example, the fact that Jesus is called the son of God implies that Jesus is divine and that it is in this divinity that he has meaning. But is Jesus' being divine the most basic and important facet of Christianity? Jesus' life, through his preaching, indicates that the Kingdom of God is actually the focal point of the Christian Church, with the divinity of Jesus assuming secondary importance.

Hence, Jesus stands for both God and man. He stands for God by fulfilling God's will, man's well-being, through his life, speech, and suffering; and yet he also stands for man in his freedom, his life with God, and ultimately his love. Finally, in his death and resurrection, he fulfilled the needs of both God and humanity. In summary, Christianity should focus on the meaning of Jesus, his life and preaching, rather than on the origin of the son of God, Jesus Christ.

The last major topic that ties together all the previously discussed topics is the Kingdom of God. The Kingdom of God is a concept very basic to the Christian faith, yet it is often misunderstood. This confusion is understandable, since Jesus Christ referred to the Kingdom of God only in analogies and metaphors, leaving theologians to interpret these often vague references. The Kingdom of God, however, may be thought of as a point in time when matter and spirit finally converge to a point of perfection.

Three basic concerns are said to be common to all humans: truth, love, and justice. Therefore, the state of perfection known as the Kingdom of God must be the achievement of perfection in truth, love and justice. There are two opinions on the way in which the Kingdom of God is reached. The first maintains that humankind as a whole is moving towards the Kingdom of God, which will be achieved here on earth. As a result, each and every one of our actions contributes in some way toward moving closer to or further away from this theoretical state of perfection. The second maintains that the Kingdom of God is seen only in death and that there is no process of evolving towards this concept. Supporters of this opinion caution, however, against believing that one is predestined to "visit" the Kingdom of God and that the Kingdom of God is the answer to man's destiny.

The first opinion envisions the convergence of matter and spirit on a large (i.e., humankind) scale, while the second envisions a more intimate (i.e., individual) convergence of matter and spirit. Which opinion should be preferred is difficult to ascertain without further in-depth study. It should be noted, however, that choosing the first creates a difficult question concerning the fate of those who die before the Kingdom of God is reached.

Proving the existence of the Kingdom of God, at first glance, seems a worldly chore, but several relatively simple proofs may be given. The best example also helps tie in the meaning of faith. This proof states that the Kingdom of God is, indirectly, the foundation on which we base our faith, and that as a consequence it gives true meaning for our existence. This argument contends that faith has no meaning if life after death (in the Kingdom of God) is not accepted as a reality. Continuing along this line of thought, we can deduce that the meaning of human existence is dependent on the existence of the Kingdom of God. A second, more mechanical proof makes use of the concept of destiny. If the existence of God is proven (an exercise in philosophy), and God is understood to have total love, then He must provide a state in which these destined people can exist—the Kingdom of God.

The concept of the Kingdom of God concludes the explanation of my personal theology which began with the investigation of the meaning of existence of self and included such important topics as Jesus Christ, God, and the church. The concept of secularization was brought out to help categorize the topic of religion, and it gave a reference point for the position of church. The question "Who am I?" brought in the concept of faith, which in turn required the explanation of the purpose of the church. Once it was concluded that the Christian Church requires the explanation of God and Jesus Christ, the concepts of faith and grace were used extensively. Lastly, the Kingdom of God was employed to show the consistency of faith, as well as to further strengthen the answer to the meaning of self. Most importantly, however, is the fact that God alone gives ultimate meaning. God is the meaning of who Greg Bohdan is.

STEVEN HAEMMERLE

IN trying to sort out my own ideas and thoughts regarding God, I first began to consider the origin of these ideas. All that I know, and will come to know, is understood through history, both my personal history and the collective history of mankind. My understanding of God is a complex and continual process of interaction between the two histories. Because the personal aspects of the man/God relationship are those with which we are most familiar, I think that our most fundamental, most primary experience of God must be personal.

Throughout history, philosophers and theologians have tried to develop arguments for the existence of God. For me to begin such a task would be foolish, for what we are seeking is not a proof of God's existence but a more mature belief in God. I believe in God because the idea of God is intuitively clear to me. This clarity is the result of my experiences in history and the awareness of God toward which they point.

Certain experiences in my life, experiences that occur in the most immediate realm of my existence, have great meaning and value for me. The transcendent meaning of the experience is something more fulfilling than the experience itself. This transcendent meaning exists somehow outside the things with which I am familiar and points toward the existence of something greater. The brilliance of a magnificent sunset causes me to reflect upon the actual beauty and meaning of the experience. The actual existence of this physical beauty is part of a more infinite beauty and it is the more infinite beauty with which I feel one. It is the sense of unity of experience and experiences, the sense of infinity that points toward an experience of God.

Friendship is another experience that has brought me to a more heightened awareness of God. I am quite aware of the special and tremendous friendships that I have developed. There is a certain bond or sameness that goes beyond our shared experiences. It is this unity, the intangible and infinite aspect of friendship, that hints toward something greater: God. It seems then, that certain experiences in our most immediate realm of existence are gateways through which our spirits can transcend, and that the infinity toward which these experiences point brings us to an intense awareness of the infinity of God.

With God's presence revealed to us in certain experiences of life, it seems logical that the harder we would look, the more aware we would be of God's presence in all experiences of life. An unlikely experience in which God can be found is in the experience of loneliness. Often I have thought, "My God, my God, why have you forsaken me?" This apparent distance from God is paradoxically a great opportunity for an even closer relationship with God. As alone as I might feel, or even want to feel, I cannot deny the God-given gift of his presence—our human ability for transcendence. In realizing the actuality of God in our Life, we are drawn closer to him; for he is always present to us.

My life then is a search for the infinite, a search for closeness with God in all my experiences. The experiences of God that I have related have all been experiences extrinsic to my being. It is through the experience of something outside my being with which I sense unity that I perceive God. At the core of our existence is God, and it is God that is meaningful for us. If, therefore, we are going to know who we are, we must know God; and it is by the transcendent experiences of things extrinsic to our being that we know God. The more I concern myself with the needs of others, the more I become aware of God; and in becoming more aware of God I become more aware of God in myself. A fundamental paradox of the man/God relationship is thus revealed. Our search for the meaning of God is a search for the meaning of our own existence.

Although our fundamental revelatory experience of God must be personal, our understanding of the man/God relationship must be a summation of both our personal history and the collective history of our community. The community history, such as that presented in the New Testament, gives insight into how others have dealt with their relationship to God. The community history is a history of God's revealing himself to mankind and thus forming a salvation history of the community. It is possible for God to be revealed to us through the revelatory experiences of others. Collectively then, our experience and the experiences of others form our knowledge of the man/God relationship as mediated by our culture. The history of this relationship is an ongoing one, and so my own relationship with God should represent the culmination of God's presence in the world to date.

I believe God exists. The clarity with which I perceive God is the result of some primary revelatory experience in my life. But how did I even come to have such an experience? It is only through the goodness of God that we

have received the self-gift of God himself. The existence
of God is utterly clear to me, because God has chosen to
reveal himself to me. As clear, though, as our understanding of God is, it still remains somewhat shrouded
in mystery.

For we, as humans, have never experienced God
directly; we have perceived him only through our experience of "something else." Be that "something else"
a meaningful friendship, the witnessing of a beautiful
sunset, or the reading of the Bible, that extrinsic experience seems to mediate the presence of God. Our
perception of God is mediated to us through all our
human experiences and therein lies the inherent mystery
of the man/God relationship.

The beauty of this relationship is that God's presence
is a total gift of himself to us. I am, however, not always
responsive to God's offer. Human existence is quite
complex, and consequently there are many concerns
with which I must contend. Being "good" is not always
so easy. A genuine love of neighbors is oftentimes very
difficult. The possibility of distance from God, or sinfulness, is a situation in which all humans find themselves. This common situation, original sin, is one in
which the occurrence of sin becomes a probability. Ex-
trication from this situation is difficult. Many times I
have tried on my own to get out of this situation. I have
found, though, that the more I get wrapped up in my
own world the further I find myself from God's
presence.

The problem with dealing with original sin on my own
is that I concern myself with only myself. The selfishness
is the most alienating aspect of original sin. I alienate

myself from both God and man. In order to overcome
the effects of original sin, one must be concerned with
the other. All this is tied up into one great paradox of
the man/God relationship. In helping others I come to a
greater understanding of God and the infinite experience of God. God's presence, grace, is mediated to me
through my concern for others. It is only through grace,
God's help, that I may extricate myself from this state of
sinfulness in the world.

In describing my experience of the man/God relationship, I have dealt thus far with issues fundamental to all
humans in every time and place. These experiences,
although fundamentally personal, speak enough of the
commonness of humanity to have relevance for all. I
have developed my thoughts on the man/God relationship as a man. I will now begin to elaborate upon my experience of this relationship as a Christian.

In order to understand Christianity, we must develop
an understanding of what it is to be human. The answer,
in part, lies in what I have already discussed. Humans
exist as thinking beings in an active relationship with
other human beings. Inherent in our being humans in relationship with other humans is our ability to experience
God, our ability to transcend. Our transcendence
toward the infinite is an end toward which all human existence strives. A human being seeks a knowledge of self
which is paradoxically found through a transcendent
and mediated experience of God. As humans we strive
to be human, and that toward which we strive is the
presence of God. Therefore, to be fully human is to be
fully graced.

The understanding of the man/God relationship is by

no means static. It is continually growing and maturing
as each generation builds upon the insight of the previous generations. As a human being living in a specific
time and place, I have a very particular comprehension
of this relationship, revealed to me most extensively
through the person of Jesus Christ. The person of Jesus
is multi-dimensional, and all aspects of his existence
have meaning. The particular emphasis placed upon different aspects of Jesus Christ is constantly changing,
and it depends upon the meaning held in value by a
given culture. Jesus is thus a reflection of the culture of
a particular place, but at the same time he has an impact
upon the culture that he reflects.

Catholic tradition has, over the ages, maintained
three dogmatic aspects of Jesus: Jesus as divine, Jesus as
human, Jesus as both divine and human in the same person. I, as a human, exist in a particular time and place,
and as such I am also a reflection of my culture. Because
of the fact that I exist in a specific context, an understanding of the complete Jesus through the human Jesus
holds special meaning for me. Jesus is not human to the
exclusion of his divinity, but rather his divinity is given
further meaning through an understanding of his humanity. An understanding of the humanity of Jesus affords incredible insight into our own humanity. For if
Jesus is really human, he must be so in a way not unlike
the way I am human.

Perhaps one of the most revealing passages from the
gospels is that passage from Luke which states that Jesus
"grew in age and wisdom." Jesus, like all of us, learned,
matured, and developed. Parallel with the physical maturation of Jesus was the maturation of his relationship

with God. Like us, Jesus possessed the inherently
human and God-given gift of transcendence. In his
development, therefore, he too must have experienced
God in the form of some mediated revelation. Jesus
struggled with the fundamentally human question of
"Who am I?" Before Jesus called others into the service
of God, he himself also experienced a call from God. As
a human being, he was unsure of what God was asking
from him. But as unsure as he was, he continued to
search for God; and his uncertainty developed into certainty. He grew to an understanding of the relationship
between man and God. As he became more aware of his
growing relationship with God, he became more aware
of who he was.

As a man, Jesus was ever transcendent and ever open
to the presence of God in his life. That toward which
humanity strives is unity with the infinite, unity with
God. For it is through the presence of God, grace, that
we come to the full realization of who we are as humans.
It is, therefore, through Jesus' infinite capacity for acceptance of God that he is at once completely human
and completely divine. Jesus gives meaning to our
humanity. It is through Jesus that we have come to
better understand the infinite capacity of the human for
God. Christ, then, is the perfection of humanity.

The implications of all this upon my life are at once
completely clear and completely unclear. It is in God
that my identity lies, and through an infinite acceptance
of God that I become fully human. The complete acceptance of God is an ideal toward which we strive, but at
which, it would seem, we cannot arrive during our
earthly existence. Is it, then, through our death that we

become fully graced beings, and as such, become completely human? And as complete human beings, are we divine? Is that what death is all about, unity with that which we call God? I myself do not know. Jesus himself was not fully aware who he was as God before his death. He was abandoned, alone, and afraid. But through his death and subsequent resurrection, he came to a complete knowledge of his divinity.

I think that the central issue of Christianity is an understanding of the duality and unity encompassed in Jesus as man and God. Through an understanding of this paradox one may come to a more complete experience of the presence of God. It is the task of the Christian, therefore, to make a conscious and serious attempt to come to as complete an understanding of this paradox as possible, even though it cannot be fully understood in this life.

All theology is faith seeking an understanding of the man/God relationship. Through an understanding of this relationship we come to an understanding of ourselves. It is thus our primary task to seek an understanding of this relationship through God's grace. Christianity affords us further insight into this relationship, for it is in the duality and unity of Jesus Christ that the man/God relationship comes to fulfillment.

A STUDENT

THE past few months have brought me to a point of crisis in my life, a time in which my personal theology has been put to the test. An entirely new, amazingly sensible approach to God has been presented to me, causing me to question my own approach to God and how much sense it really makes. The major difference between my theology and that given in class can be characterized by the example of an iceberg. As a child I was presented with the tip of the iceberg and told that it was my religion and that I was expected to follow it faithfully. This new theology, however, begins at the base of the iceberg and works toward an understanding of the tip, that which was originally handed to me as my religion.

I have a difficult time justifying our traditional "box theology," and yet I cannot simply throw it out the window. Habits are difficult to break, and I am afraid that this is what my faith has become over the last twenty-one years. Although the approach that we have taken in class makes much more sense, simply adopting it in the span of two months' time would seem thoughtless, like reducing my faith to a whim or a fluke. In other words, I cannot simply adopt a new theology without critically examining it and relating it to my own life and experience. Essentially, I am caught in the middle, torn between two modes of thinking, the sensible and the habitual.

The following is a formulation of my personal theology as it stands today, a culmination of my thoughts over the past few months. I will address the ideas of faith, revelation, grace, original sin, Jesus Christ, and the death of Jesus, and attempt to give them some kind of meaning in my life. Since each idea seemed to logically progress from one to the other in class, I shall adopt this same order in presenting my own thoughts.

I mentioned that my faith has become habitual, basically a routine which I follow every Sunday and holy day. I am ashamed to admit it, but over the past six years or so, my so-called "faith" has been a show, an act put on to appease those around me. There has really been no faith there at all. Over the years I have attended mass because I was afraid of the consequences if I did not go. Missing mass would place even more sin on my soul, and I already felt myself in "hot water" because of my poor attitude toward God and the Catholic Church in general. I did not want to make my situation any worse.

I guess I might also have continued going to mass hoping for some kind of divine inspiration, something to eliminate the awful thoughts and feelings I experienced. I honestly felt I was an evil person because of these feelings and that I would eventually end up in hell. Come to think of it, I can remember asking God on several occasions to please rid me of all the doubts I had because somehow it had been conditioned into me that doubt was evil. I really do not think I will ever know if this idea was self-inflicted or if it was conditioned in me as a youth by those around me. It is not important now anyway.

Why is it not important? Last February was the first time I really ever confronted my "faith," mainly because for the first time, faith itself was presented in a different frame of reference. Faith is something we gradually build through years of questioning and hours of reflection. The more we can fit faith into our experience, the stronger our faith becomes. But what exactly is meant by "fitting faith into our experience"?

The best way I can explain this is by showing how "box faith" fails to fit into human experience. For those of us who were handed faith, how do we explain our knowledge of God and his deeds? Basically, stories were relayed to us from the Bible about God, Jesus Christ, etc.; and we accepted them as being true. We were told, however, that it did not matter whether the stories were true or not, because with faith there was never any question.

Faith, in this respect, never touched our lives as humans. It was always a mystery. Worse yet, it had no foundation. It was built from nothing. In other words, we could not justify our faith through our own experience.

Now, however, faith is justifiable through human experience. After hours of reflection, I have justified my faith in the following manner. To begin with, I realize that my life is an endless search for who I am. I am never really satisfied. I always want to know more. The amazing thing is that I never realized this until the notion was presented to me as a question: Do we ever stop growing as human beings? Are we ever ultimately satisfied? The answer is "no," and it is "no" for all humans. This endless search for ultimate satisfaction is the foundation for my own faith today. I am confident that some day, somewhere, I will discover complete satisfaction. Based on human history, though, I can safely assume that the majority of us will not experience this satisfaction as human beings. Whether it comes at or after death, I cannot say. Even if I were confident that it does occur, for example, at death, I could never be absolutely sure. It is not really important for me to know when satisfaction comes anyway. The confidence that it will come is all that matters.

Now some may argue (as my roommate did) that this type of faith is just as much a mystery as our "box-faith." The distinction I make lies in what I term a "tangible mystery." My faith today is a tangible mystery. I work every day toward resolving this mystery, and every day I learn more and more about myself and the world around me. I can feel myself getting closer and closer to whatever it is out there that I search for.

This is the key to my entire faith. I have come to an understanding and an acceptance that what is out there is ultimately God. When I look at my situation from this point of view, it seems impossible to deny that there is a God. Granted, the representation of this God is a very individualistic, very personal matter. God is different for each and every one of us. Our individual experience paints our own portrait of God. The notion I wish to convey, though, is that there is a God for each and every one of us. We have to understand and accept this God through our own personal reflection and not by the command of others.

Now that my faith in God has a foundation, I will begin to build on it. Many aspects of faith were discussed in class, some of which were more difficult to understand than others. God's revelation seemed to be one of the more difficult to fit into my own experience, mainly because revelation is a matter of pure interpretation.

On the other hand, the principle of mediation—God's presence to us and action upon us through secondary causes, persons, places, events, things, nature, history —seems applicable to all human experience. This is exactly what we mean when we speak of transcendence. These secondary causes are our "pipeline to God". By reaching beyond these persons, places, events, etc., we can bring ourselves that much closer to what we are searching for—that is, God.

Just think about it. How else could God possibly communicate with us? In the context of my own experience, there is no other way. My understanding is that God is communicating with me constantly, regardless of whether I recognize it or not. It is easiest to see my point in reference to a jigsaw puzzle. The puzzle is not identifiable until all the pieces have been put together. Analogously, if we have not yet figured out God's message, it is because more of the pieces or details are yet to come. Once we have all the pieces, if we ever do, we will understand God's message. This poses an interesting question. That is, do we ever really acquire all of the pieces, or does the puzzle just continually grow, requiring an endless number of pieces?

I have not yet found an answer to this question. At times I seem to receive messages from God. For example, I know when I should or should not have done something or said something. If I had to pinpoint it, I would say that my emotions are my best link to God's message. At other times, though, I feel myself waiting for some kind of guidance from God and never seem to get it. Confusion has a strange way of intensifying my impatience. I can recall times when I have sarcastically

said to God, "Thanks a lot for all your help, Buddy!"
As you can see, the question of whether there is a limit
to the number of pieces in the puzzle is a tough one to
answer. It would take me more than a few hours of reflection to thoroughly resolve it in my mind.

God's gift, like his message, was difficult to justify
from my own experience. I had never really reflected on
God's grace because, quite frankly, I never knew what it
was. To me, grace was just a word they used at mass,
usually mentioned in the context of "God's saving
grace." My previous impression was that God's grace
would be bestowed on me if I was a "model" Catholic.
In essence, I always thought that a Catholic had to earn
God's grace. In our new methodology, though, nothing
could be further from the truth.

How then, can grace be understood through human
experience? The fact that God's grace is a gift cannot be
stressed enough. This gift is present with us at all times.
Just as we can feel the presence of someone we love with
us at all times, so we explain the presence of God.
Through the people around us, the people we love, we
slowly come to realize that God is present every day in
our lives.

Another misconception I had concerning grace was
that it was suddenly bestowed on us by God. One
minute we were without it, the next we had it. But
accepting or rejecting God's grace is not an explicit
event that can be isolated in a person's life. It is a result
of many experiences, of everyday living. In fact, for
most, it probably takes a lifetime to fully know of God's
grace.

Grace, then, is put on a more personal level when we view it from our human standpoint. It gives a glimmer of hope to those of us who seriously questioned the existence of a God, and to those who still question the laws of the church. I am secure in the understanding that God's grace will always be there for me. I never had this type of security before because, unfortunately, our "box faith" never seemed to allow for doubt or confusion.

There are many other aspects of faith that require justification, but from a human standpoint original sin seems to be the one of most concern. Why? Because we are all sinners no matter how hard we try not to be. How then do we explain sin in the world today?

I tend to agree with the thought that we are what our relationships with others make us. We are born into this world without any knowledge or any consciousness that would enable us to decide for ourselves from the beginning. We are exposed to sin through our relationships with others from the day of our birth. We do not have the power to reject it because we have no knowledge of its existence. We have no indication that this sin is affecting us; and, worst of all, we have no way to avoid it.

It was proposed in class that original sin probably exists today because God's grace is not at our disposal in the manner and to the degree that God intended. I think a more appropriate reason is that we, as humans, are not as open to God's grace as we should be. Our lives today are an endless search for a formula for happiness and success. Is it possible that this search is overshadowing

our search for God's grace? I believe this is the case for
many of us today. We are caught up in this mode of survival, always trying to keep our heads above water.
Most of us have not realized the full power of God's
gift. Yet the stronger the realization of what God's gift
is, the less we have to worry about our predicaments as
human beings. It is this offer of hope that relieves the
burden of sin. So the stronger our understanding of
what God offers to us, the less we are burdened by sin.

Up to this point I have attempted to explain my
understanding of the faith I have and some of its many
outgrowths. Everything has been relatively logical, able
to be reasoned through with minimal concentrated effort. Now I have come to the most difficult aspect of
Catholic Christian faith around today—the understanding of Jesus Christ, the Son of God.

The teaching of the church has always been that Jesus
was both fully human and fully divine. Can this possibly
be justified in the light of our human experience? How
do we interpret the New Testament stories and gospels?
Do we take them as historical accounts or as purely symbolic?

My understanding of Jesus Christ throughout my life
was always based on the fact that Jesus was humanly
divine. So much emphasis was placed on the divinity of
Christ (such as the miracles he performed) that I lost
sight of the fact that Jesus was just as human as the rest
of us. I had always been told that it was a matter of faith
as to whether the gospel accounts of Jesus' life were true
or not. If I had faith, I should never have had reason to
question. But, once again, my faith had been based on
nothing. There were those who said the Bible accounts

were fact, and there were those who proposed that they were just stories written by a believer for a group of believers. Who was right and who was wrong?

The understanding that I have now is that neither was right or wrong. Whether or not Jesus Christ actually performed all the miracles attributed to him is not important. Whether or not Jesus was crucified is not important. The important thing to remember is that Jesus Christ had a mission that he believed in, a mission to spread the news that the Kingdom of God was at hand. Jesus had an understanding of God which he felt compelled to share with all mankind. His need to spread this word of God was so powerful that he was unable to see the danger that eventually led to his death. What is most important for us to remember is that Jesus died for the sake of all men. He died in hopes that what he could not convey to the people through prayer and teaching, he could convey through his own death.

How does Jesus Christ fit into my own life today? Karl Rahner's approach has been the most logical formulation of Jesus Christ I have encountered to date. Rahner considers Jesus as a human being first and foremost. We naturally can fit this type of Jesus into our own experience. We can understand his compulsion, his sorrow, and his determination, because we have all experienced each of these at times in our lives.

Also, the idea of a human Jesus giving up his life for us had more meaning, at least for me, than that of a divine Jesus doing the same. I feel closer to a Jesus who was human, a Jesus that actually feared death. How can anyone not identify with a Jesus such as this?

Throughout the last few months, I could not help but

feel anger toward the fact that I was never presented with this alternate view of Christianity. The many doubts I had were frustrating—actually causing me to lose what little faith I had. I also have never reflected so intently on so many aspects of my religion. It is amazing how little I actually understand. If anything, I have learned to reason with myself. I realize now that if I question a doctrine, I am not obliged to accept it. My only responsibility is to work with it until I reach a solution that is acceptable to me, and only me.

AFTERWORD

Andrew M. Greeley

"AND so there sits my seashore, just as I am sure there is one for every person on this earth. It is evolving, constantly and I along with it. For now I am seated on dry land just dangling my feet in the water—only to become completely submerged after I pass out of this world."

Thus does Maureen Hartnett end the account of her own personal theology at the conclusion of Father David Murphy's course in the theology of Karl Rahner.

How many such young women and men are there in the country like these Golden Dome Rahnerians? Are they typical or merely an isolated phenomenon?

The truth is, I suspect, somewhere in the middle. The young "theologians" in these essays are on the one hand part of a highly select group—men and women at Catholic colleges who choose to take a course from a demanding teacher about a German theologian of whom many had never heard before. On the other hand they are probably no more different from their age peers than were those who would take an optional theology course a quarter century ago. Typical? No. But a "sign of the time" for their generation? Surely.

There would almost certainly be more of them if there were more professors of theology like Father Murphy.

It is generally assumed by wise persons in the American Church that the postconciliar generation of young people is both less devout and less Catholic than those who moved through the early phase of their life cycle before the Vatican Council. The changes in the Church, the crises in society in the late sixties and early seventies, the so-called "sexual revolution"—all are supposed to have produced young Catholics who are poorly trained in their faith and not loyal to their church.

Try as I might, however, I can find no evidence to support this wisdom in my sociological research. Do young Catholics of college age reject the Church's sexual ethic on birth control and pre-marital sex? So do their parents and in about the same proportions.

Does their religious devotion mark them as an inherently less religious group of age cohorts than their predecessors? It would seem not. The trend lines project church attendance when they are in their forties as exactly the same as that of those who are presently in their forties. Young women and men born after 1945 are no different in the projected patterns of their church attendance through the life cycle than are those born during the Depression and the War. Cohort, as we sociologists would say, does not improve the goodness of fit of a life cycle model. In simpler language, age affects church attendance, when you were born does not.

This finding is so counter-intuitive to many priests and parents that they deny the possibility it could be true. My only response is that such people should collect their own data and fit their own models.

Moreover, work which Professor Michael Hout of the University of California at Berkley and I have done indicates that it is primarily religious loyalty which keeps Catholics coming to Church regularly. We can find no evidence that such loyalty has decreased among the postconciliar generations.

To those who also reject as patently false the concept that younger Catholics are as loyal as their parents and grandparents (and our data leave no doubt about that) I would say that loyalty does not have to be expressed with the same style in all times and all places.

Moreover I have found a profound change in the religious sensibility of the postconciliar generation—their religious imagination is more likely to emphasize the affectionate, tender, intimate aspects of the human/God relationship. At first many are tempted, like Father Raymond Schroth S.J., to dismiss images and pictures of God as phenomena which are etherial, fluffy and irrelevant (what, asks Father Schroth, does a madonna's smile have to contribute to the search for justice and peace?). However, a "graceful" religious imagination is the only measure of religion available to us which correlates positively with political and social attitudes and behaviors—voting, help for the poor, racial justice, respect for civil liberties, opposition to the death penalty, concern about the nuclear arms race.

On balance then, a case could be made that the generation of Father Murphy's students is at least as religious and quite possibly more religious than its predecessors— as loyal, as devout, more socially concerned, and more "gracious" in their images of God.

With these empirical findings at hand, one is not so

surprised by the men and women who struggle through Karl Rahner under Father Murphy's direction. They represent the first postconciliar generations. While their style of Catholicism may be different from that of the preconciliar generations, it does not follow that their Catholic substance has deteriorated. On the contrary, it may well have improved. No, all of them are not as thoughtful, as reflective, as skilled at linking experience and doctrine as are Father Murphy's students. Yes, his students do indeed point at the religious concerns, the style of religious expression, and the direction of religious tendencies in their own generation.

The great merit of the late Karl Rahner's theology is that it linked experience with doctrine, despite some Catholic reactionaries who think that religious experience and doctrine—poetry and rationality—are inherently opposed. The great merit of Father Murphy's course, as its results are manifested in this book, is that he has made the Rahnerian method available to young men and women whose religious style demands that they learn how to reflect intelligently on their experiences of grace.

In the present impoverished condition of religion and theology teaching, it would seem that very few young Catholics are taught the required sensitivity to their own experiences and the equally essential disciplined intellectual method necessary to reflect on their experiences. Jeremiads about "liberation," "peace and justice," and "the third world," frequently substitute for such training, mostly because the teachers, in a monumental loss of nerve, have abandoned faith in the validity of their own or their students' experience of God and all confidence in theological methods which are not immediately "relevant" or even "revolutionary."

One has the impression that high school and college students discount such enthusiasms the way in a former era their predecessors discounted enthusiasms about devotion to the Sorrowful Mother Novena or the the importance of the Fatima Secret.

I am convinced by my empirical data that the method of theological education which Father Murphy proposes will be far more effective at producing Catholics concerned with "peace and justice" than the insensitive and undisciplined harangues of the Sisters (Fathers and Brothers) Mary Ignatius of our time.

Moreover I am also convinced that the method, suitably adapted by a creative and well-educated teacher, can be applied all the way down to the junior high school level. In my occasional classes with CCD students here in Tucson I have found that it is a very easy matter —if one abandons the "lecture at" style of both the Old and the New Church—to persuade young women and men to talk about and reflect on their experiences of God and grace. They may not always come up with the "right" answers. The teacher must be brave enough, as Father Murphy certainly is, to run that risk.

But almost always, like Father Murphy's Rahnerian Fighting Irish, they are sane enough to ask the right questions.

In the words of Anne Monastyrski, "It is my ability to

love which reveals to me the human capacity of transcendence and immanence. Once I recognized that my
parameters are set—and they are set at the Infinite—
than I am ready to journey towards the Kingdom where
the journey ends, when I reach Reality.''

Andrew Greeley
Tuscon
Holy Thursday, 1985